THE ANCIENT
NEAR EASTERN
TRADITION

MAJOR TRADITIONS OF WORLD CIVILIZATION
UNDER THE EDITORSHIP OF HAYDEN V. WHITE

THE ANCIENT NEAR EASTERN TRADITION

MILTON COVENSKY

Associate Professor of History
Wayne State University

HARPER & ROW, PUBLISHERS

NEW YORK AND LONDON

Library of Congress Catalog Card Number: 66-20795

C-1

CONTENTS

v

EDITOR'S INTRODUCTION

It was once customary to refer to the ancient Near East as the cradle of civilization. And it used to be thought that all of the higher civilizations of the world, including that of China, were offshoots of the ancient Near Eastern type. Scholars no longer credit this diffusionist theory of civilizational growth; most now believe that mankind emerged from primitivism and entered into civilization at about the same time in many different places of the world. But interest in ancient Near Eastern civilization has not diminished; it still provides the best documented example of the elements and processes in early civilizational genesis.

In his contribution to this series—Major Traditions of World Civilization—Professor Milton Covensky has tried to characterize the basic pattern of the cultural experience of the entire ancient Near East. His was the most difficult assignment of the series, for he not only had to deal with some three thousand years of history, many different peoples, and two major cultural streams—the Mesopotamian and the Egyptian—he also had to show how they fused during the second millennium B.C. to form that cultural amalgam against which the Hebrews, the Greeks, and the Romans defined their respective contributions to world civilization. Hebrew, Greek, and Roman cultural forms seem more familiar to us than those that descend from the ancient Near East, and they seem familiar and original to us precisely in the degree to which they differ from their more "Oriental" counterparts in Mesopotamia and Egypt. But in reality much of what passes for an original creation of the Hebrew, the Greek, and the Roman people originated with peoples much older than they in the lower Mesopotamian and Nile valleys. For the ancient Mediterranean world, the Near East *was* the cradle of civilization. And although the Hebrews, the Greeks, and the Romans did succeed in breaking the pattern of cultural behavior they inherited from the ancient Near East, they borrowed as much as they rejected from that older cultural heritage.

Western man has always been fascinated by the apparent stability and durability of Mesopotamian and Egyptian cultural traditions. The Greeks and the Romans confronted the Near East with something amounting to awe; they were inclined to attribute the longevity of Mesopotamian and Egyptian institutions to some special wisdom, some unique understanding of the world process, peculiar to "Orientals." Much of this Greek and Roman attitude has come down to modern times, but contemporary scholars are inclined to attribute the stability and longevity of ancient Near Eastern civilization to a combination of environmental and intellectual factors that naturally rendered the peoples of Mesopotamia and Egypt suspicious of change and innovation. The institutions, ideas, and values of the ancient Near East were adequate to the sensed needs of human life in that part of the world at that time. Order and security—the marks of civilization—could, in the ancient Near Eastern world, very easily appear as a gift of the gods rather than a creation of man; and the peoples of that world saw no reason to place them in jeopardy by gambling on an imagined better life than the one they had.

Professor Covensky defines Mesopotamian and

Egyptian civilizations as both archaic and primary. By primary he intends their originality, their immediate relation to earlier primitive stages of cultural growth, and their relative independence from other higher civilizational traditions. While recognizing that in the course of their development both civilizations borrowed much from other peoples, he is interested in defining the extent to which they were original creations of the peoples of the areas in which they appeared. By archaic he intends the main direction of their cultural aspiration, their tendency to relate everything in their daily lives to the original experiences of their ancestors in bringing order and security out of the chaos of primitive existence. Unlike the Hebrews, who looked both backward and forward in their attempts to provide an explanation of what was happening to them in their own lived present, the archaic peoples looked backward only. They experienced the future with the hope that things would not get worse than they had been in the past. New experiences, new ideas, values, and practices won their way into the conscious part of their lives only with the greatest difficulty and after the longest period of association. Such an attitude is decreasingly characteristic of modern men who, in the face of every disaster, continue to bank on the inevitable amelioration of the human condition. But this archaic attitude was justified in the ancient Near East, given the stability of the physical environment and the slow pace of technological development after the New Stone Age.

The central cultural experience of the ancient Mesopotamians and Egyptians was the way in which they related to the great rivers, which—if properly worked—provided them with the luxuries and necessities of civilized existence. The different features of the Nile on the one hand and the Tigris-Euphrates complex on the other are reflected in the cultural institutions that took shape in their valleys during the third millennium B.C. Though similarly life-providing, the power of the Tigris-Euphrates was much more difficult to harness than that of the Nile. And Mesopotamian climate and geography did not inspire the kind of confidence in the beneficence of the universe which soon emerged as a distinctive characteristic of the civilization that grew up on the banks of the Nile.

Professor Covensky shows how the more erratic and violent tenor of life in the Mesopotamian river valley was reflected in a more pessimistic world-view, and how this pessimism was reflected in turn in the religion of the Sumerians, the original organizing people of the area, and their descendants. He then shows how the Sumerian conception of the gods and men's relation to the gods led to the creation of distinctively *political* institutions, such as the city-state, kingship, and written law codes. These institutions were political, and differed from their Egyptian counterparts insofar as they were conceived to be administered *by men*, even though they were administered *on behalf of the gods*. The recognition that men were responsible for order and security gave to Mesopotamian culture a flexibility and innovative power that was lacking in Egypt. In Egypt it was assumed that the gods ruled directly over the land through one of their own number, the pharaoh. If institutions were created by the gods and administered by them, it had to be assumed that they were perfect and that any flaws in their operations were due to failures on the part of men, not of the system itself. If, on the other hand, it was assumed that mere men were governors, it was possible also to believe that men ought to better themselves, their laws, and their institutions by systematic reform. And in the progressive revisions of the great law codes of Mesopotamia we have evidence of the innovative power of this pessimistic world-view—this, in spite of the fact that every revision was presented as a return to the purity of the origins, rather than as an advance into an essentially different future.

The stability, beneficence, and order of nature as it appeared to men in the Nile valley were reflected in Egyptian religion in a kind of boundless optimism that promoted belief in a life after death, the goodwill of the pharaoh, and the conviction that whatever was, was right. In his presentation of the Egyptian notion of Ma'at (justice) and of the central position of sun worship in Egyptian religion, Covensky suggests the abiding sense of the sanctity of order and regularity in all aspects of human life. And in his discussion of Egyptian architecture, sculpture, and painting, he shows how this sense of order and regularity found expression in material and symbolic form.

Thus, Covensky begins by showing both the similarities and the differences between the two main components of ancient Near Eastern civilization. On the one hand, they shared a common archaic attitude towards change, a desire to relate everything to the primal experience of their ancestors, who had given them the gift of an orderly and secure existence. On the other hand, they viewed with completely different affective predispositions the task of maintaining and prolonging that order and security. For the Mesopotamians, civilization was recognized as a precarious achievement, as something that might be withdrawn at any time by the fickle gods who ruled over them and whose slaves they were. For the Egyptians, civilization was a marvelous bounty which they were charged to enjoy in return for service to the sustaining gods, represented by the pharaoh.

Having outlined the main differences and similarities

of the original forms of the two cultural traditions, Covensky then turns to the story of how they became fused and
amalgamated. This process of fusion is discussed under
three headings: (1) the period of conflict between Egypt
and the Hittites, which followed upon the first great incursion of Indo-European barbarians ca. 1800 B.C.; (2) the
age of small nations (Philistines, Phoenicians, Arameans,
Hebrews, etc.), which lasted down to about 900 B.C.; and
(3) the age of new empires (Assyrian, Chaldean, and
Persian), in which the old cultural forms were revived and
systematically sustained as part of a program of cultural
regeneration for the entire Near East. Here the emphasis
is on continuity, on the ways in which old forms were filled
with new contents by peoples who came as conquerors,
but were themselves taken captive by the institutions and
values of the peoples they conquered.

The assimilation of new peoples by the Egyptians
and Mesopotamians was not easy. Both regarded their
homelands as being in some sense chosen, and they
resented the intrusions of alien peoples with strange gods
as falls from the primal state of purity willed to them by
their ancestors. But the Egyptians and the Mesopotamians
were given to a mode of thinking that promoted in them,
in the long run, a kind of broad practical tolerance. Professor Covensky calls this mode of thinking mythopoeic,
and he sees it as linking the world-view of the primary
archaic civilizations with that of primitive times and dis-
tinguishing this world-view from that of the secondary
civilizations, such as the Hebrew, Greek, and Roman, which
broke with the mythopoeic mode.

Professor Covensky's discussion of mythopoeic thought
is necessarily brief, but he gives many examples of how it
functioned in both Egypt and Mesopotamia to provide the

peoples of those areas with some understanding of the world process. Some additional remarks here may help to point up some of the aspects of mythopoeic thought that Professor Covensky's examples suggest.

Prior to about a half century ago, it was thought that a myth was a childish form of reasoning at best and a conscious invention, a fraud, or a lie at worst. Now it is generally held that myth is rather a kind of *unconscious* invention, an attempt to provide a meaningful, though non-scientific, explanation of experiences that are incomprehensible to the available science of an age or epoch. What myth does is relate an experience that is unfamiliar to one that is familiar by revealing the purpose behind it in terms of human emotional needs, interests, and desires. Thus, for example, a natural event such as a flood, a thunderstorm, or an earthquake is regarded not as a result of impersonal natural forces, but as a manifestation of some spiritual force that is similar in its activating principles to the kinds of impulses that activate living men. Generally, a myth explains a given set of events by relating them as parts of a story in which specific ends or purposes are realized. These ends and purposes are conceived to be similar to such emotions as love, hate, desire, envy, and the like, which everyone recognizes as components in his own spiritual disposition. The purpose of myth is not to make life more bearable, but to make it comprehensible by providing a human meaning for it. Thus, myth is a kind of coding device, the effectiveness of which is to be judged by its success in identifying the world with the processes of human consciousness. Its critical standards are psychological rather than objectively compelling, and its aim is to provide any explanation in place of no explanation at all. And it does this by translating new experiences into familiar experiences, by showing that there is really nothing new under the sun.

Now, although mythopoeic thought does not lead to greater control over the physical world in the way that scientific thought does, it at least has the effect of making the world appear to be less strange to man and allows men to assimilate new experiences to received bodies of information and knowledge. It is true that mythopoeic thought does generate a certain hostility to anything that does not admit of easy assimilation to received traditions. but it at least requires that the new and different be confronted as a problem rather than as a miracle. Thus, when the cultural traditions of Egypt and Mesopotamia came into conflict during the second millennium B.C., and each of these cultures was forced to confront the fact that it was not the sole center of the world, mythopoeic thought provided a strategy by which this new condition could be assimilated. And, as Professor Covensky shows, there occurred a general homogenization of cultural forms that bore rich fruit in the cosmopolitan and tolerant civilization of the Persian Empire.

It was this civilization which the Greeks had to confront in the sixth century B.C. and which the Romans finally conquered in the first century B.C. The absorptive powers of this cosmopolitan culture were still vital and effective even at that late date. And though the Romans conquered the Near East and made it a part of their own world empire, the traditions of that part of the world remained strong and pervasive even under Roman rule. Further, as Covensky notes, when the Romans had to choose between the Western and the Eastern halves of their empire, they chose the latter as the more worthy of defense and salvation. By the fourth century A.D., the Roman Empire had itself become transformed into an "Oriental" monarchy; it had adopted a political system, a religion, and a style of life that were distinctively Near Eastern. The ancient Near Eastern tradition thus proved itself stronger in that time than the Hebrew, Greek, and Roman traditions, which had tried to break away from it—a tradition that perdured into the Middle Ages in Byzantine and in those aspects of Muslim culture that continue to influence the world even today.

HAYDEN V. WHITE

March, 1966

CHRONOLOGY

The student should take careful note that (1) experts on the ancient Near East frequently do not agree among themselves on chronology, and (2) that no dates are certain for the ancient Near East before the tenth century B.C.

MESOPOTAMIA

Prehistoric Cultures—Southwestern Asia

ca. 75,000 B.C.	*Food-gathering stage*—characterized by free-wandering hunters and the beginnings of tool-making.
ca. 60,000 B.C.	*Food-gathering stage*—characterized by restricted wandering, hunting, and more variety in standardized tool forms; some regional variety, e.g., in Iraq and Kurdistan.
ca. 35,000 B.C.	*Food-collecting stage*—characterized by groups who practiced restricted wandering seasonal collecting, and selective hunting; appearance of blade-tool tradition.
ca. 10,500–8500 B.C.	*Suspected food-producing stage*—possible plant and animal domestication along flanks of Zagros mountains; presence of flint sickles, milling stones, mortars, pestles, etc., point to domestication.
ca. 6750 B.C.	*Food-producing stage*—rise of primary village-farming community, village community of Jarmo—rectangular houses, obsidian trade, domestication of wheat, barley, possible domestication of dog, goat, sheep, and pig.

ca. 6000–
5000 B.C.

Food-producing stage—further elaboration and spread of the village-farming type of community at Hassuna and Samarra; painted pottery style of Samarra; cultural merging on a large scale.

ca. 5000 B.C.

Food-producing stage—Halafian. Centered in northern Mesopotamia; arose in Assyria, extended south to Samarra; effective food-producing may also have been introduced at this time in southern Mesopotamia; probably invention of wheeled vehicles, primitive textile industry.

ca. 4250–
3750 B.C.

Food-producing stage—Ubaid. Witnessed the beginnings of urbanization—towns with temples plus smaller settlements—extended over a wide range of southwestern Asia, but focus was in southern Mesopotamia.

Protoliterate Cultures—ca. 3750–3000 B.C.

Centered around peasant *Uruk* and more advanced *Jemdet Nasr* cultures. Decisive creation of writing on clay tablets, beginnings of ziggurats, cylinder seals; expansion of cities in central and northern Mesopotamia; probable cultural impact on Egypt (cylinder seals and brick buildings).

ca. 3000–
2371 B.C.

Early Dynastic Period of Sumerians. Centered in Sumer; struggles between temple city-states (Ur, Erech, Larsa, etc.).

ca. 2371–
2113 B.C.

Akkadian Interlude. Political control in hands of Semitic Akkadians. Sargon the Great (ca. 2371–2316 B.C.); union of all Mesopotamia under his control.

ca. 2113–
1792 B.C.

Sumerian Revival. Third dynasty of Ur (ca. 2113–2006 B.C.). Invasions of seminomadic Semites called Amorites into Mesopotamia.

ca. 1792–
1758 B.C.

Hammurabi. Union of Sumer and Akkad into single kingdom; bilingual use of Akkadian and Sumerian; Babylon becomes chief city

	of Mesopotamia; Code of Hammurabi; further fusion of Smerian and Semitic elements; high civilization.
ca. 1600–1100 B.C.	Kassites establish Third Babylonian Dynasty. Threaten the successors of Hammurabi; aided by Indo-Europeans, take possession of Babylon.
ca. 1500 B.C.	MITANNI EMPIRE (at its height).
	Hurrians, Indo-Iranian superstructure of chariot-warriors, center of Empire in middle Euphrates, dominate Assyria.
ca. 1310–1232 B.C.	FIRST ASSYRIAN EMPIRE.
883–612 B.C.	SECOND ASSYRIAN EMPIRE. Able rulers: Ashurnasir-pal II (883–859 B.C.), Tiglath-Pileser III (745–727 B.C.) Sargon II (722–705 B.C.), Sennacherib (705–681 B.C.), Esarhaddon (681–668 B.C.), Ashur-bani-pal (668–625 B.C.). Assyrian Empire eventually includes Mesopotamia, Elam, parts of Iran and Asia Minor, Syria, Palestine, and Egypt.
612–539 B.C.	NEO-BABYLONIAN, or CHALDEAN EMPIRE. Chaldeans rule over Mesopotamia, Syria, and Palestine; Nebuchadrezzar, king from 605–562 B.C., destroys Jerusalem in 586 B.C.

EGYPT

Prehistoric Cultures

ca. 200,000 B.C.	*Food-gathering stage*—no fossil human remains yet found in Egypt; earliest tools of Abbevillian and Acheulean types, such as egg-shaped bifaces.
ca. 10,000 B.C.	*Food-gathering stage*—last phase of Old Stone Age in Nile, known as Sebilian; progressively smaller tools (microliths); beginning of geometric forms; food remains in form of bones of buffalo, wild ox, and mounds of *Unio* shells.

ca. 4500 B.C. *Food-producing stage*—in Upper Egypt known as Tasian; in Lower Egypt, as Fayum "A." Mainly pottery remains from Tasian.

ca. 4000 B.C. *Food-producing stage*—in Upper Egypt, known as Badarian; in Lower Egypt, as Merimda. Badarians had agricultural villages, cultivated wheat and barley, raised pigs, goats, and sheep, used the plough and hoe, baked bread. Employment of copper; good pottery with figurines. Badarian culture shows affinity with other African cultures.

ca. 3600 B.C. *Food-producing stage*—in Upper Egypt, known as Amratian, a predynastic culture. More intensive cultivation of Nile River valley. Amratian villages organized as clans with animal totems such as crocodiles. Utilization of black-topped stone jars and red-burnished pottery.

ca. 3300 B.C. *Food-producing stage*—known in Upper Egypt as Gerzean, a predynastic culture. Pottery employed red designs on a buff ground; increase of population; initial attempts at irrigation and draining; much use of copper; Mesopotamian impact (cylinder seals and brick buildings); thorough farm economy.

Dynastic Periods

ca. 3200– THINITE PERIOD. *First and Second Dynasties.*
2700 B.C. Creation of writing; unified kingdom of the two lands; concept of Ma'at and divine kingship.

ca. 2700– OLD KINGDOM. Consolidation of theocratic
2200 B.C. rule; sacred society and state; elaboration of bureaucracy; development of funerary architecture culminating in pyramids.

ca. 2700–2650 B.C. *Third Dynasty.*
King Djoser (ca. 2700 B.C.); great archi-

tect, Imhotep, designed and constructed mortuary complex at Sakkarah, step pyramid.

ca. 2650–2500 B.C. *Fourth Dynasty.*
King Snefru (ca. 2650 B.C.), construction of regular pyramid at Meidum. King Cheops, or Khufu (ca. 2600 B.C.), the "great pyramid" of Gizeh. King Chephren (ca. 2560 B.C.), giant pyramid. King Mycerinus (ca. 2525 B.C.), smaller pyramid.

ca. 2500–2350 B.C. *Fifth Dynasty.*

ca. 2350–2175 B.C. Pyramid Texts.

ca. 2350–2200 B.C. *Sixth Dynasty.*
King Pepi I (ca. 2325 B.C.)
King Pepi II (ca. 2275–2185 B.C.)

Signs of disintegration with increasing power of monarchs. Old Kingdom ends with death of Pepi II.

ca. 2200–
2050 B.C.

FIRST INTERMEDIATE PERIOD. Extends from *Seventh through the Tenth Dynasties.* An age of great disorder and chaos.

ca. 2050–
1800 B.C.

MIDDLE KINGDOM. Celebrated *Twelfth Dynasty* (ca. 1990–1780 B.C.), looked upon by later Egyptians as their classical age. Vast public works such as irrigation project in the Fayum.

ca. 1800–
1550 B.C.

SECOND INTERMEDIATE PERIOD. *Thirteenth through Seventeenth Dynasties.*

ca. 1730–1570 B.C. Hyksos rule in Egypt.

ca. 1570–
1090 B.C.

NEW KINGDOM
   EGYPTIAN EMPIRE
ca. 1570–1305 B.C. *Eighteenth Dynasty*
   Thut-mose I (ca. 1525–1495 B.C.)
   Thut-mose II (ca. 1495–1490 B.C.)
   Thut-mose III (ca. 1490–1436 B.C.)

              Hat-shepsut (ca. 1486–1468 B.C.)

              Amenhotep II (ca. 1439–1406 B.C.)

              Amenhotep III (ca. 1398–1361 B.C.)

              Amenhotep IV (ca. 1369–1353 B.C.)

                  Creates a religious "revolution," and changes name to Akhenaton, establishes new capital city Akhetaton, movement fails.

              Tutankhaton (ca. 1352–1344 B.C.)

                  Changes name to Tutankhamen, abandons Akhetaton, returns to Thebes, signifies the failure of Atonism.

ca. 1150–663 B.C.	Post-Empire Period. ca. 715–663 B.C. Ethiopian Period.
663–525 B.C.	Saitic Period. *Twenty-sixth Dynasty.* Temporary political and spiritual recovery.
525–404 B.C.	*Twenty-seventh Dynasty.* Persian domination. Cambyses until Darius II.
404–398 B.C.	*Twenty-eighth Dynasty.*
398–378 B.C.	*Twenty-ninth Dynasty.*
378–341 B.C.	*Thirtieth Dynasty.*
341–333 B.C.	Second Persian Domination.
332 B.C.	Conquest by Alexander the Great.

HITTITES

ca. 2000 B.C.	Settle in Asia Minor.
ca. 1400–1200 B.C.	HITTITE EMPIRE. Under King Suppiluluimash (ca. 1380–1347 B.C.). Hittites conquer inner Asia Minor and possibly to the Aegean; to the east he extended the empire to Armenia and Assyria. Conquered by sea peoples around 1200 B.C.

ARAMEANS, HEBREWS, AND PHOENICIANS

Arameans

A Semitic nomadic people who since ca. 3000 B.C. had settled on the Middle Tigris.

ca. 1080–880 B.C.	Have opportunity for independence and expansion conflicts with Assyrians.
	Established themselves on right bank of Euphrates and to the south beyond Damascus.
732 B.C.	Assyrians regain upper hand and conquer Aramean kingdom.
	Land caravan traders and role of their language, make them important.

Hebrews

ca. 1000–960 B.C.	David and Early Hebrew Kingdom.
ca. 973–933 B.C.	Solomon.
933–722 B.C.	Northern Kingdom of Israel.
933–586 B.C.	Southern Kingdom, or Judah.
535 B.C.	Cyrus of Persia grants Hebrew exiles the right to return to their land.

Phoenicians

ca. 1200 B.C.	Become independent in form of city-states after Hittite decline.
1100–800 B.C.	Phoenician states prosper.
774–625 B.C.	Phoenicians politically fall victim to Assyria.
	Phoenicians importarnt as colonizers, sea traders, cultural intermediaries—spread of alphabet.

PERSIA

705–550 B.C.	Medes in Persia.
550–331 B.C.	PERSIAN EMPIRE.
	546 B.C. King Cyrus (550–529 B.C.) defeats Lydians.
	538 B.C. Captures Babylon.
525 B.C.	King Cambyses conquers Egypt.
521–486 B.C.	King Darius controls an empire reaching from the Nile in Egypt to the Indus River in India. Ancient Near East is now in the hands of Persian rulers.

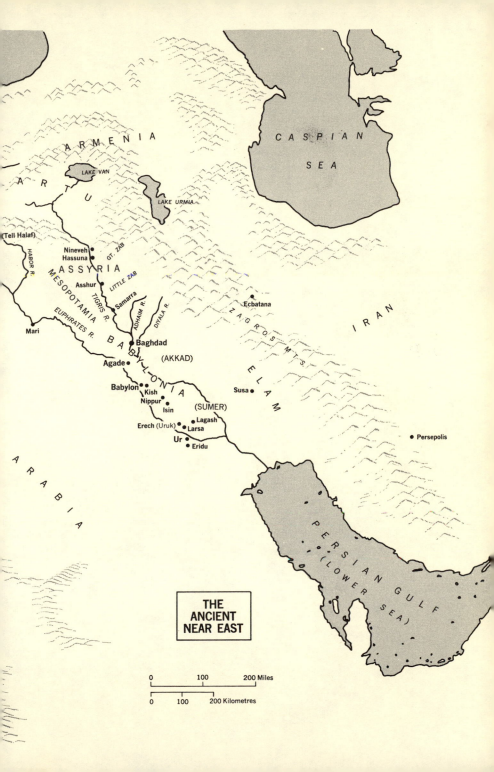

THE
ANCIENT
NEAR EAST

THE RISE OF PRIMARY ARCHAIC CIVILIZATIONS IN MESOPOTAMIA AND EGYPT

The Twentieth Century and the Ancient Near East

During the last hundred years the entire history of the ancient Near East has been reconstructed, re-examined, and reinterpreted, and that process is still in full swing. From our standpoint in mid-twentieth century we can see that the historian has profited from three intellectual achievements that have made possible a total reassessment of ancient Near Eastern civilization. These are, first, remarkable advances in archaeology; second, a new understanding and appreciation of the role of myth and ritual in archaic societies; and third, a better understanding of the importance of technological-social forces in history. These three achievements give us a clearer understanding of the rise, development, and transformation of ancient Near Eastern civilization and illuminate an important segment of history.

1

Egyptian and Mesopotamian archaeology have benefitted from a larger archaeological revolution which began in the nineteenth century and has accelerated in our own time. Today, interest in archaeology is greater than ever before, and the field of archaeological study is in remarkable ferment. This revolution is a product of a number of factors. These include, first, an expansion of the historical consciousness of Western man. In this respect archaeology is comparable to psychoanalysis. For just as psychoanalysis represents an expansion and broadening of man's mental dimension by revealing underlying layers and hidden recesses of the mind in the unconscious, so archaeology constitutes an attempt to enlarge his historical dimension by revealing the underlying layers and hidden recesses of his most remote historical and prehistorical experiences. Both psychoanalysis and archaeology attempt to disclose past experiences long hidden or forgotten, but which nevertheless exercise a significant influence. In both areas there is a preoccupation with origins—psychoanalysis investigates the primitive origins of the psyche while archaeology probes into the archaic origins of civilization. And both the psychoanalyst and the archaeologist attempt, each in his own fashion, to reconstruct on the basis of partial and fragmentary evidence a picture of the sequence of development.

Secondly, archaeological investigation, in the Near East especially, has grown out of a desire of Western man to find a larger framework for the biblical narrative—to place the Bible more accurately within its wider Near Eastern setting, to check, and where possible confirm, the biblical narrative by archaeological findings. Many biblical scholars were convinced that the only way to understand the Bible was to discover how it resembled and

differed from the ideas and institutions created by other
ancient Near Eastern peoples. To achieve this, a deeper
knowledge of the ancient Near East and its archaeological
foundations was required. Thus, it is no accident that
biblical scholars have contributed to the archaeological
revolution in the Near East.

Thirdly, archaeology has received a powerful stimulus from certain developments in natural science. Indeed, its methods have in many instances been revolu-
tionized by the application of techniques of analysis
developed in other disciplines ranging from electronics to
biochemistry. New methods, such as radiocarbon and
obsidian dating, the dating of pottery by thermolumines-
cence, pollen analysis, and the application of optical emis-
sion spectroscopy to the study of metallurgy in the Bronze
Age, are examples of the fruitful union of natural science
and archaeology.

Fourthly, the archaeological revolution expresses
the universal interest in the problem of civilization which
has developed in our time. The comparative study of civilizations, ranging far afield to explore peoples distant in
space and time, has left its impact on archaeology. Investigations are thus not limited to any one area but have
become global. Archaeological expeditions are scattered
over all continents; Africa, Asia, the Americas, Europe,
and Australia are parts of a worldwide orbit of investigation. Indeed, even an underwater archaeology has
emerged, and the great seas themselves are now subject
to the probing hands, eyes, and instruments of this science.

Finally, the growth of archaeology as a distinct discipline has contributed to the revolution. The employment
of hundreds of specialists, numerous learned journals, re-
fined techniques, and sophisticated methodologies has had

a self-accelerating effect upon this revolution in our time. When one remembers that up to the nineteenth century, archaeological interest in the Near East was almost non-existent with the area's ancient history founded mainly upon biblical tradition, superficial knowledge of a few Egyptian monuments brought to Europe, and the vague reports of travellers, the achievements of Near Eastern archaeology seem truly phenomenal. Yet it must always be borne in mind that the results of archaeological investigations at any particular moment are tentative and not final.

Even as archaeology functions as an indispensable aid to the understanding of the ancient Near East, so too has twentieth-century comprehension of myth and ritual enriched our knowledge of ancient Egypt and Mesopotamia. The search for the meaning of myth is much older than the twentieth-century. The nineteenth century created the so-called science of comparative mythology and in the process accumulated an enormous amount of material on the myths of different times and places; nevertheless, a profound difference exists between the way myth was interpreted prior to the twentieth century and the way it is understood in our time. Up through the nineteenth century, the prevalent view was that myth constituted a kind of fable or fiction, an invention, a story with no truth to it and therefore possessing an essentially illusory character. But more recently myth has assumed a new positive meaning. Instead of seeing it as a form of illusion, scholars now see it as a form of knowledge or expression, as a way of looking at the world. Anthropologists, psychologists, and philosophers now attempt to understand how myth actually functioned in primitive societies and archaic cultures. As the distinguished anthropologist, Bronislaw Malinowski, expressed it, "myth as it exists in a savage community, that is, in its living primitive form, is not merely a tale told but a reality lived. It is not in the nature of fiction such as we read today in a novel but it is a living reality, believed to have once happened in primeval times, and continuing ever since to influence the world and human destinies."

In archaic civilizations such as Egypt and Mesopotamia, myth functioned to create a way of experiencing the world, in a manner that was sacred in its tradition, primordial in its revelation, and exemplary as a model for both gods and men. Mircea Eliade, a leading historian of religion, thus arrives at the following comprehensive notion of myth:

> Myth narrates a sacred history; it relates an event that took place in primordial time, the fabled time of the "beginnings." In other words myth tells how, through the deeds of Supernatural Beings, a reality came into existence, be it the whole of reality, the Cosmos, or only a fragment of reality—an island, a species of plant, a particular kind of human behavior, an institution.

In the twentieth century a whole corps of scholars has attempted to draw the implications of this newer notion of myth. They have addressed themselves to problems such as the structure of mythopoeic thought,[1] the

[1] In this book the term "mythopoeic" is used in preference to the term "mythical." "Mythopoeic" always has reference to the active process of creating myths or of experiencing the world in a mythical fashion. The term is derived from two Greek words, *mythos* (myth) and *poiein* (to make). The student should note that when we say that the ancient Egyptians and Mesopotamians engaged in mythopoeic activities, we do not mean that they were incapable of other forms of thinking, such as the logical-mathematical and empirical-technological. The high attainments of Babylonian mathematics, science, and practical arts reveal a capacity to think and function on many different levels.

relation of myth to ritual, the application of the concept of myth to religion, anthropology, literature, history, psychotherapy, and art. This group of scholars includes philosophers such as Ernst Cassirer, anthropologists like Bronislaw Malinowski, Melville Herskovits, and Clyde Kluckhohn, historians of religion such as Mircea Eliade, Samuel Hooke, and E. O. James, psychotherapists such as Sigmund Freud and Carl Jung, and literary critics such as Stanley Hyman and Northrop Frye, to cite only a few. And, especially for the area of the ancient Near East, the late Henri Frankfort, together with some colleagues at the Oriental Institute at Chicago, has produced notable studies of the pattern of myth and ritual in ancient Near Eastern civilization. Numerous other works on the same topic have been undertaken. While these scholars have not always agreed, the newer twentieth-century concept of myth unquestionably throws a significant light on many aspects of human culture and on ancient Near Eastern culture in particular.

At the very time the twentieth century was arriving at a more comprehensive notion of myth, it was also independently acquiring a larger understanding of the role of technological-social forces in history. In modern industrial-technological society, problems of power, rationality, urbanization, bureaucratic regulation, invention, and social organization have taken on much greater significance. The social sciences have become highly self-conscious and articulate with respect to these issues, and historians and other social scientists now look at the past with these problems in mind. Thus archaeologists such as V. Gordon Childe have stressed the role of material factors and technological changes in the rise of civilizations in the ancient Near East. In a symposium conducted by the Oriental

Institute of the University of Chicago, entitled *City Invincible* (1960), leading orientalists discussed the connection between urbanization and cultural development in the ancient Near East. They frequently sought to apply ecological and sociological analyses to the historical material, but with uneven results. Because technological-social factors play such an overwhelming role in contemporary society, the danger always exists that the historian will overstress their significance for the ancient Near East. Nevertheless, employed in moderation, the analysis of technological-social forces is a useful tool in the study of the ancient orient.

To summarize—the findings of numerous twentieth-century scholars in archaeology, mythology, and the analysis of technological-social forces provide us with a basis for a wider comprehension and deeper understanding of the ancient Near East.

Factors in the Rise of Primary Archaic Civilizations in Mesopotamia and Egypt

The appearance of the primary civilizations in Mesopotamia and Egypt in the fourth millennium B.C. constituted a new and unprecedented development in human history. Mesopotamian and Egyptian civilizations each took on a unique identity and way of life, but both civilizations were based on the presence of large permanent communities with their own traditions and unity of distinctive religious values. Both civilizations made use of elaborate political and bureaucratic organization, highly specialized occupations, systems of writing, trade and commerce, and monumental architecture on an unprecedented scale.

Both civilizations were preceded by a sequence of prehistoric cultures that archaeologists have painstakingly unearthed.[2] The two civilizations utilized and undoubtedly depended upon certain technological achievements from the prehistoric past—for example, the domestication of plants and animals, which accompanied the Neolithic Revolution. Both Mesopotamia and Egypt had a prehistory, and while that prehistory was a necessary prerequisite for the emergence of the two primary civilizations, it is not of itself a sufficient explanation. For the rise of Mesopotamian and Egyptian civilization constituted a leap, a breakthrough, an emergence of genuinely new ideas, institutions, and values.

How was it possible for the first primary civilizations to get a start in ancient Mesopotamia and Egypt? What caused them? Innumerable attempts have been made to answer this question but it must be frankly confessed that historians have not yet worked out any answer that does not bristle with thorny problems. Were solely indigenous factors responsible for the two civilizations, or were common causes at work in both areas? Are there general causes for the rise of all such primary civilizations as Mesopotamia, Egypt, China, and India, which demand a comparative study? These and hundreds of lesser questions vex the historian and admit of no ready solution.

We mention four attempts to solve the problem, merely to indicate the variety of answers proposed. The famous historian Arnold Toynbee in his *Study of History*

2 The term "prehistoric" refers to times when there was a lack of writing, no high civilization, and relatively small communities. In historic times high civilizations appear and make widespread use of writing, constitute large communities, and have an awareness of historical belonging and identity.

rejected race and environment as the critical factors in the geneses of civilizations. Instead he argued that all of them, including Egypt and Mesopotamia, were responses to challenges of particular difficulty which force men to make a hitherto unprecedented effort. A great civilization will never arise, according to Toynbee, if the challenge is either too easy or overwhelmingly difficult. For Toynbee, then, the key lies in a combination of physical, social, and psychological forces.

The eminent archaeologist, Gordon Childe, on the other hand, found the key to the rise of primary civilizations in material factors alone. In a series of books including *Man Makes Himself* and *What Happened in History,* Childe stressed the importance of a surplus of wealth and population which accompanied the rise of villages. Out of the surplus of wealth came a ruling class, while specialized artisans were drawn from the surplus of population. Villages gave way to larger urban communities which utilized bureaucratic and other techniques and led to the establishment of primary civilizations.

In his book, *The Origins of Civilized Societies,* however, historian Rushton Coulborn rejected both Toynbee's and Childe's explanations. Instead, Coulborn named religion as the main factor in the creation of primary civilizations because it provided society with a basic unity and purpose. Finally, the late Henri Frankfort, a great orientalist, in *The Birth of Civilization in the Near East* expressed genuine doubts that the causes for the rise of primary civilizations in the Near East could ever be ascertained.

The lack of a clear-cut solution to the problem of the origin of civilizations indicates how complex and involved it is. In this brief account all that we can do is call attention to some of the necessary preconditions for the emergence of high civilizations in the ancient Near East. The sufficient cause or causes still elude the historian.

Prehistory and the River Valleys

The primary civilizations with which we are concerned arose in the river valleys of the arid subtropical zones of the ancient Near East. Some promising leads as to the causes of the beginnings of high civilizations in these areas have taken place in recent decades with the creation of a "new" archaeology led by such scholars as Robert J. Braidwood and Robert M. Adams, both of the University of Chicago. In contradistinction to the "old" archaeology which concentrated its major efforts on the excavation and restoration of ancient ruins and the collection of individual artifacts, the "new" archaeology seeks to recover whole settlements of past populations. It not only tries to reconstruct these past communities but to examine ecologically how man functioned in relating to the available plant and animal environments. The cultural-ecological approach has solidly established itself among American archaeologists. Thus, in a recent symposium entitled *Courses Toward Urban Life* (1962) Braidwood and a number of other scholars examined sixteen different areas of the world in an effort to determine the several patterns which led from food collecting to urbanism. With Bruce Howe of Harvard University, Braidwood dealt specifically with southwestern Asia beyond the Mediterranean coastal region.

Several aspects of their approach are worthy of interest. First, they have for the most part abandoned the traditional scheme of classifying man's preliterary or prehistoric past on the basis of materials used for stones and weapons. Terms such as the Old Stone Age or Paleolithic, New Stone Age or Neolithic, a mixed Copper-Stone Age or Chalcolithic, a Bronze and Iron Age, are deemed inadequate and confusing. Instead, Braidwood and his colleague offer a new general course of cultural development for prehistoric southwestern Asia. It began about 75,000 B.C. with a food-gathering stage and free-wandering hunters who use standardized tools made by flaking and the like. This was followed by a food-gathering stage with more restricted wandering, hunting, and some variety in tool forms (ca. 60,000 B.C.). Then came a food-collecting stage with selective hunting and seasonal collecting patterns (ca. 35,000 B.C.). Following this phase from about 10,500 to 8500 B.C.) there emerged a food-producing stage with some kind of plant and animal domestication along the flanks of the Zagros Mountains. By about 6750 B.C. a food-producing phase with a primary village-farming community was present at a site called Jarmo in northern Mesopotamia, characterized by some long-range trade in obsidian, domesticated wheat and barley, and, possibly, the domestication of the dog, goat, sheep, and pig. Braidwood and Howe then postulate a series of phases which further developed and spread the village-farming way of life (ca. 6000 B.C.) into Mesopotamia. Finally, they speak of a food-producing phase—the Ubaidian Period, roughly between 4250 and 3750 B.C., which was characterized by incipient urbanization in that it had towns with temples. The focus of the Ubaidian Period was southern Mesopotamia.

In their approach Braidwood and Howe distinguish a whole series of "environmental zones" in southwestern Asia, one of them being the Tigris-Euphrates river valley south of Baghdad. They reject environmental determinism and therefore oppose any notion that changes in climate or natural environment occurred between about 12,000 and 8000 B.C. to bring about the crucial change from food collection to food production. They show indeed that the first village settlements were not located in the river valleys at all, but in the hill country.

Despite the establishment of a sequence of cultural phases from early food gathering to incipient urbanization, Braidwood and Howe have not as yet given an adequate explanation for the transition from village-farming communities to temple towns. Moreover, there is still a qualitative difference between the Ubaidian Period and the succeeding Protoliterate Period which began with the invention of writing and an awareness of historic civilization. In short, the cultural-ecological approach has filled in many necessary gaps, but it has as yet not answered the crucial question: Why did high civilizations emerge in the river valleys proper, particularly in southern Mesopotamia?

THE TIGRIS-EUPHRATES VALLEY

The importance of the river valleys calls for a closer look at the geography of Mesopotamia and Egypt. The name Mesopotamia means "the land between the rivers," and is used in this context to designate the entire region between the Tigris and Euphrates rivers, extending from the Kurdistan highlands in the north to the Persian Gulf in the south. Today this area is part of the Republic of Iraq.

The Tigris and Euphrates rivers have their sources in the mountain country of northern Armenia. Both rivers, together with their tributaries, carry enormous amounts of sediment which is deposited along their southerly or lower courses. Southern Mesopotamia from Samarra to the Persian Gulf is a low-lying plain roughly 400 miles long and 125 miles wide, formed of deposits of silt from the two rivers; and the lower reaches of this plain was the seat of a primary civilization in Mesopotamia.

At Samarra, agricultural production depended upon rainfall. South of Samarra, the cultivation of crops was made possible by the annual inundation of the two rivers. Each year in late spring, between April and June, the rivers overflowed. Since rainfall was extraordinarily scarce in the south, the overflow was of life-giving significance.

Four features of the inundation should be noted. First, the inundation was annual and appeared to be part of a lunar-solar calendrical cycle. Second, the timing of the annual overflow could not be pinpointed by the Mesopotamians because the floods depended on weather conditions in the far-distant mountains of the north, where the snows melted. The coincidence of heavy rains in the northern areas and snow in the Zagros and Taurus mountains frequently resulted in inundations that wreaked savage destruction. The overflows were not gradual, but sudden and precipitous. Moreover, the rivers occasionally changed their courses, which in a number of instances caused the destruction of entire cities. Third, the annual overflow could be regulated, however, by a system of irrigation and drainage; and fourth, the soil was enriched by the deposit of silt from the overflows.

Each of these features had a significant impact on the primary civilization which emerged in the Tigris-Euphrates river valley. Without the annual inundation no such civilization would have arisen in the low-lying and otherwise arid plain. Yet what impressed the ancient Mesopotamians most was not the periodicity of the inundation, but its violently erratic character and unpredictability. Since no one could tell precisely when the flooding would come, the Mesopotamian considered the flood to be the enemy of man. Ninurta, the Sumerian god of the inundation, who was also a god of war, was not regarded as a beneficent god, but as a malevolent one; in the later epic of creation of the Babylonians and Assyrians, entitled *Enuma Elish,* there is depicted a giant battle between the god Marduk (or Enlil), representing the winds, and the goddess Tiamat, the water. In a powerful victory Marduk kills Tiamat by crushing her body and cutting her arteries. The winds then carry her blood away. This portion of the myth seems to be rooted in an ancient Mesopotamian interpretation of the spring floods. In this interpretation the waters that overflow the low-lying plains revert each spring to the primeval watery chaos, which is then conquered by the winds, thus permitting the land to dry. But the identification of the annual flood with the primeval watery chaos gave a permanent stamp of evil to the inundation.

The uncertainty, violence, and unpredictability of the annual floods are mirrored in the most basic Mesopotamian attitudes towards life—a sense of its uncertainty and the basic insecurity of the cosmos itself. The Mesopotamian view of man and the world was fraught with anxiety and concern. Unlike the Egyptian, who was confident and usually optimistic, the Mesopotamian was basically pessimistic and often consumed by anxiety. He was never certain about his relations to the flood, to his fellow men, and to the divine powers, and he was anxious about what awaited him in the afterlife. Man's weakness and insignificance before the great powers that surrounded him perpetually haunted the Mesopotamian, giving a distinct quality to Mesopotamian civilization from start to finish.

The Mesopotamian was confronted with the perennial and hopeless task of overcoming the uncertainty inherent in the universe, the gods, men, and the flood. He saw himself as having perpetually to satisfy and propitiate the gods so that their decisions would favor him. One of the ways he could do this was by sacrifice and prayer. Another was to employ functional-technological means. The Mesopotamian probably did not distinguish between the two as we do, but of the efficacy of the second method there can be no doubt. It was of critical importance, for Mesopotamian civilization would have been impossible without the intricate system of irrigation and drainage which flourished there in the third millennium B.C.

Two differing views have been offered regarding the nature of early Mesopotamian irrigation. One position is represented by Sir Leonard Woolley who holds that large-scale irrigation systems were introduced at the start of the civilization and shaped the political systems of the early temple city-states. Woolley's argument is that the Euphrates riverbed was higher than the surrounding plain. This necessitated a system of perennial irrigation, which yielded two harvests but required much labor. Canals from the high river had also to be high, the main canals being as much as 25 yards in width and feeding a system of subsidiary canals inland. Drainage canals also had to be provided. All this involved communal labor, cooperative efforts, and centralization of control. And Woolley contends that "the Euphrates delta was from the outset parcelled out into a number of agricultural irrigational units each having its own centre of administration, and the development of the city-state was due not to the peculiar mentality of the Sumerian people but to the physical character of Sumer."

Another view, advanced especially by Robert Adams, denies the initial use of large-scale irrigation. Instead, Adams holds, the pattern in Mesopotamia had already been utilized late in the fifth millennium in numerous villages and towns of the Ubaid culture. These communities made use of short canals which branched off from nearby river channels. Large-scale irrigation was introduced in Sumer only after the "process of political integration into territorial states was well under way." For Akkad, north of Sumer, it was introduced even later. Since in this particular instance, towns do exist before the appearance of large-scale irrigation works, Adams' position appears the more tenable of the two.

Whatever the system initially employed, large-scale irrigation eventually prevailed. Irrigation in any form enriched the soil and facilitated agriculture. Plowing in the plain was greatly aided by the flat terrain and the absence of stones. However, the soil of the Tigris-Euphrates river valleys was always attacked by salt brought in both by irrigation and ground water. Initially this salinization was not a problem but eventually it became serious, and even in ancient times the productivity of the land was decreased, thereby contributing to declining prosperity.

One final aspect of the geography of Mesopotamia contributed to the sense of insecurity of its people. Unlike Egypt, Mesopotamia was frequently subject to invasions and attacks from all sides. Nomads from the deserts to the south and north had to traverse no significant natural barriers to carry out their raids on the cities of the Mesopotamian plain. Mesopotamia was open to attack from Iran, Armenia, Anatolia or Asia Minor, and Syria, so her people had to struggle for existence against both the gods and man. Little wonder that they were pessimistic in their

basic attitude and exceedingly grateful for whatever success they achieved.

THE NILE VALLEY

In Egypt, a river valley also played a vital role in
the emergence of civilization. One of the ancient
Egyptians' designations for their country was the "Red and
the Black," and this was quite appropriate. The red represented the desert hill area, similar in climate to the great
Sahara, while the black stood for the narrow fertile valley,
one to twenty-four miles in width, that extended like a
ribbon the length of the Nile.

Had it not been for the Nile, the land of Egypt in
historical times would have been almost nothing but desert.
The river, over 4000 miles long, rises in equatorial Africa
among such lakes as Victoria and Albert. This White Nile,
as it is known in its upper course, has a vital tributary, the
Blue Nile, which rises in the mountains of Abyssinia. The
Blue Nile joins the White Nile at Khartum, approximately
1350 miles from the Mediterranean Sea, whence the river
winds its way through Nubia, in a difficult and tortuous
path into Egypt. The river has slowly cut its way through
the Nubian sandstone. In six places, though, the Nile chan-
nel is partially interrupted by rocky formations, known as
cataracts, which make transportation difficult.

Below the first cataract at Aswan, the Nile enters
Egypt proper where, in the course of time, it has cut its
way through the northern desert limestone plateau. There
it has created a long valley trench, extending in width from
ten to thirty-one miles, which constitutes Upper Egypt.
About one hundred miles from the Mediterranean, the

Nile has formed a triangular territory which the Greeks called the Delta and which constitutes Lov: · Egypt. The Nile flows through the Delta in two branches, reaching the Mediterranean at a western mouth called the Rosetta, and an eastern one named the Damietta.

Each year, beginning in June, the Nile overflows. This overflow is caused by the Blue Nile, which carries melted snow and spring rains and sediment into Egypt. The waters and deposits of the Nile created a fertile soil in the valley and also gradually built up the Delta. The peak of the inundation is reached in the fall. Unlike Mesopotamia, where the timing was unpredictable, sudden, and frequently ferocious, the inundation in Egypt was gradual and exactly predictable. While the Mesopotamian looked upon the flood as man's enemy, the Egyptian regarded it as a blessing and salvation. The Egyptian god of the flood, who embodied the spirit of the Nile, was called Hapy, a beneficent god, "whose coming brings joy to every human being."

Isolated in his valley and blessed by an annual inundation that was both gradual and predictable, the Egyptian viewed the world with an abiding sense of security and optimism, in striking contrast to the Mesopotamian.[3] The Mesopotamian was distraught over the harshness and ferocity of the world, but the Egyptian was impressed by its kindness. The deserts to the east and west of Egypt, the harborless coast of the Delta, and the precipitous cataracts to the south, all provided the Egyptian with a degree of geographic isolation and protection which allowed him to believe that all the forces of the universe

[3] This is not to deny that in times of turmoil like the First Intermediate Period (ca. 2200–2050 B.C.), the Egyptians voiced pessimism. But these were exceptions rather than the rule.

were conspiring to render him secure and safe from every harm, social as well as physical.

In Egypt, as in Mesopotamia, the annual inundation required some type of irrigation, but the Egyptian system differed from the Mesopotamian. The early Egyptians developed a basin irrigation system by which the areas of cultivation were divided into many earthen rectangular troughs with sides of wall-like banks and with the soil as a floor. At the time of the inundation, the overflow waters entered these basins, where they thoroughly soaked the soil and deposited a layer of silt.

This system required only a series of local basins which could be separately maintained by individual villages. In short, large-scale irrigation efforts involving the collective cooperation of cities or the central state were unnecessary. The eminent Egyptologist John Wilson has therefore suggested that the absence of a genuine urban life in early Egypt may be rooted in this basin type of irrigation. He has also denied that the initial unification of Egypt was the result of large-scale irrigation efforts by the state. On the other hand, some other Egyptologists still insist that irrigation is the clue to the creation of a centralized, orderly, unified Egyptian state. Whether it came first or later, one foundation of Egyptian, as well as Mesopotamian, civilization must be looked for in its conquest of the life-giving waters of its great river.

ARCHAIC MESOPOTAMIAN CIVILIZATION

The civilizations of ancient Mesopotamia and Egypt were both primary civilizations; that is, they were not derived from or affiliated with other earlier high civilizations. Instead, the antecedents of both were a series of distinct prehistoric cultures. The roots of Mesopotamian civilization extended back at least to the Tell Ubaid culture which flourished around 4000 B.C. Sometime between 4000 and 3000 B.C. Mesopotamian civilization entered upon a period of gestation designated as the protoliterate and predynastic phases. In earliest times, a people called the Sumerians played a leading role in Mesopotamia, and in two periods, the early dynastic period of the Sumerians (ca. 3000–2371 B.C.) and the Sumerian Renaissance (ca. 2113–1792 B.C.), Mesopotamian civilization assumed an increasingly distinctive form. Two of its features are of extraordinary interest and significance. They are its great duration and its "substantial uniformity throughout its long career." Let us take a closer look at these two interrelated factors.

Mesopotamian civilization endured for over 3000 years. Despite the Medes' conquest of Nineveh in 612 B.C. and the Persians' capture of Babylon in 539 B.C., the basic pattern of the civilization persisted. Indeed, even after the conquests of Alexander the Great in 331 B.C., and the creation of Hellenistic empires, Mesopotamian civilization retained many of its characteristic features.

This persistence over such a long period of time is all the more remarkable when one takes note of the wide diversity of peoples who swept into Mesopotamia and sought to exercise partial or total control over it. Unlike Egypt, Mesopotamia was continually subjected to invasions by motley linguistic, racial, and ethnic groups. The most famous were the Sumerians, the Babylonians, and the Assyrians, but there were many others including the Gutians, the Kassites, the Chaldeans, the Hurrians, and the Elamites. The natural assumption would be that invasions by such diverse groups would bring radical changes and basic discontinuities in the culture. But instead of changing the basic pattern of Mesopotamian civilization, these groups were all assimilated by it.

This is not to assert that changes did not occur. There were innumerable modifications in detail, and many of these were of some consequence. But the overarching uniformity of Mesopotamian civilization outweighs these differences in detail. As the noted expert on Mesopotamian civilization, Ephraim A. Speiser, put it, "The over-all structure remains uniform and self-consistent." And Speiser notes that if one approaches Mesopotamian civilization in the large, "the cultural constants outweigh the chronological variables."

The span and uniformity of the civilization were related to a third feature, namely its archaic character. It was remarkably resistant to basic change, and a principal reason seems to have been that it was absorbed with the problems of origins. Archaic civilizations were not preoccupied with the future or with problems of change or development. Instead, they always sought to maintain links with their sources or beginnings. The archaic civilizations assumed that the world was ready made at the beginning of time. They were thus dominated by the notion that the great events had already happened in primeval times and continued thereafter to influence the world and human destinies.[1]

According to this notion, the significance of anything is to be found, not in its end, but in its primordial beginnings. This is why myths of creation loom so large in Mesopotamian civilization. And this is possibly why Mesopotamian civilization was so indelibly stamped by its creators and originators—the Sumerians. Of course another important reason why so many peoples adapted to the basic pattern of Sumerian civilization was that the new groups became literate only by learning cuneiform and copying the old texts as standard pedagogical activity. The significant thing is that the Mesopotamians made Sumerian culture a norm and standard, with the result that the Sumerian achievement in such areas as writing and religion left a permanent mark on all subsequent Mesopotamian civilization.

Sumerians and Semites

Who were these Sumerians? To this day historians disagree as to their origins and are only in substantial accord that they were invaders and not original dwellers in

[1] The student should not confuse the terms "primary civilizations" and "archaic civilizations." "Primary" refers to civilizations that are not affiliated with previous high civilizations but proceed

Mesopotamia. Their language bears no relationship to either the Indo-European or Semitic families of languages. In accordance with their mythopoeic way of looking at the world, the Sumerians believed that they had lived in Mesopotamia since the very creation of the world. They called their country Shumer. Modern historians designate it as Sumer, the most southerly part of Mesopotamia. North of Shumer was Uri, which is known by historians as Agade or Akkad, named after the capital city established by the Semitic ruler, Sargon the Great. The territories of Sumer and Akkad together constituted the stage for the opening act in the drama of primary Mesopotamian civilization.

In the third millennium B.C., Sumer comprised about twelve separate city-states. These included Ur, Erech, Larsa, Lagash, Kish, Isin, and Nippur. Such city-states consisted of a city proper, which was usually walled, and its surrounding territory. Frequent warfare raged as these city-states struggled for leadership. At times a powerful conqueror would appear to subdue a number of them and temporarily create a larger political unit. But after a relatively brief time the territory of Sumer would again be divided into independent and contending units.

An early king of the city-state of Kish, Etana, may have temporarily established himself as the ruler of Sumer and neighboring lands as early as 3000 B.C. Shortly thereafter, the city-states of Erech and Kish exerted their power. For a time, in the early dynastic period, Ur became the leading capital city of Sumer, but Erech reasserted itself

---

from prehistoric roots. Archaic civilizations are civilizations that "normatively" regard all their great events as having happened in primeval times and which continue thereafter to influence the world and human destinies. Mesopotamia and Egypt were both primary *and* archaic civilizations.

under a powerful ruler, Gilgamesh, who became the legendary hero of the famed Epic of Gilgamesh.

Such constant warfare was bound to weaken the political power of the Sumerians. The result was an interlude extending from about 2371 to 2113 B.C. during which the city-states lost political control to the Semitic Akkadians. The Semites—peoples in the ancient Near East who spoke Semitic languages—were seminomads, using donkeys. (The camel did not become a major transport animal until around 1100 B.C.) Therefore, most early Semites lived on the edges, the arable land and the grazing land around established cities. The Semites north and west of Sumer, led by a brilliant ruler, Sargon the Great, (ca. 2371–2316 B.C.), established a new dynasty of Semitic rulers. Sargon united all of Mesopotamia under his control and may have extended his rule into Syria and Asia Minor. He made Akkad the capital city of his empire and accelerated the absorption of the civilization of the Sumerians in Akkad. The boast was made that Sargon was king of the known world and ruled over the four quarters of the earth, a boast that remained as an ideal for future Semitic rulers. Under Sargon's grandson, Naram-Sin, however, the attempt to maintain the empire failed. A semibarbaric people from Iran, the Guti, overran Sumer, plundering and destroying. The result of this incursion was that the city-state of Akkad was permanently devastated and disappeared from history.

Between ca. 2113–1972 B.C. the Sumerians attempted a revival and reconstituted themselves in Sumer. Once again, individual Sumerian city-states took the initiative, with Lagash and its ruler, Gudea, playing a leading role. A struggle also ensued between the cities of Lagash and Ur, with Ur emerging as the victor, and the third dynasty of Ur was created, lasting over a century from 2113 to 2006 B.C.

Meanwhile, Semitic seminomads called Amurru or Amorites moved into Mesopotamia. The Amorites seized control of such cities as Larsa, Babylon, and Isin, and even succeeded in finally capturing Ur. For the next two hundred and fifty years, bitter warfare raged between the cities of Isin and Larsa and between Larsa and Babylon. These struggles ended around 1792 B.C. when the Babylonian ruler, Hammurabi (1792–1750 B.C.), established himself as the sole king over Sumer and Akkad.

An outstanding warrior, Hammurabi, united into one kingdom the numerous city-states of Sumer and Akkad. The whole land was given a single language, a Babylonian dialect of Akkadian, for administration and business. Sumerian continued to be the language employed by the priests in their liturgies. Babylon became the greatest city of Mesopotamia, with Marduk its chief god. Hammurabi was also significant as an administrator and lawgiver. Under him, Semitic and Sumerian elements in the culture fused harmoniously. Although Semitic-speaking peoples were now everywhere in control in both Sumer and Akkad, and the Sumerians as a people had disappeared. Mesopotamian civilization continued to be strongly Sumerian in both form and spirit.

The tangible achievements of early Mesopotamian civilization from the time of the Sumerians through the reign of Hammurabi are truly impressive. They include the creation of the city-state and the establishment of an urban civilization which rested on agriculture; the concept of a sacred state ruled by a god through a king; a complex economic life based on a division of labor, a merchant class and a money economy; the utilization of legal codes; the establishment of bureaucracies; the technological mastery of irrigation systems of canals, dikes, low dams, and reservoirs; technological skill in agriculture; the use of copper and bronze; building in brick; an elaborate art; a mathematics based on the sexagesimal system but attaining to the solution of complex quadratic equations; the development of a cuneiform system of writing; a varied literature; the elaboration of schools and education; and a vast proliferation of religious ideas and institutions.

Mesopotamian Institutions and Beliefs

This early Mesopotamian civilization rested upon a strange marriage between functional-technical achievements and a sacred, religious, mythopoeic outlook. To the Mesopotamians—Sumerians and Semites alike—the sacred mythopoeic outlook was of supreme importance, but the presence of various functional-technical achievements such as the control of irrigation and agriculture, the deployment of military power, and the utilization of bureaucracies, were equally necessary bases for the development of this primary civilization. It must be borne in mind that whereas in modern Western civilization, religious factors are subordinated to the functional and technical, in archaic Mesopotamia the situation was basically reversed. Functional-technical factors were often absorbed under the larger aegis of a sacred religious world outlook by the Mesopotamians.

Thus, for example, we tend to view warfare as a secular activity that has little or nothing to do with religion. Not so with the Mesopotamians. The Sumerians regarded wars between the various city-states as wars between the different city gods, and when a city was victorious, this signified that its god was more powerful than his rival. Though each city obviously took practical steps to defend itself, the Mesopotamian, within his scheme of basic values, did not believe that success in warfare finally depended on such measures. Instead, he held that success ultimately depended on the favor of the gods.

The same was true of irrigation. On the one hand, the Mesopotamian exercised great skill and patience in developing a technology of irrigation. On the other, all these means were subordinate, in his estimation, to the willful pleasure of the malevolent god of the flood, Ninurta. In the last resort, all human contrivances depended on the favor of the gods.

The difference between the modern Western and ancient Mesopotamian views of institutions can be well illustrated by that vital institution of early Mesopotamia, the city-state. To modern Westerners, including their historians, the city is a secular institution created by man to minister to human needs. It is subject to development and change. To the Sumerians the situation was basically different. In order to understand how the Sumerians regarded the city one must grasp two basic notions—the idea of archaic mythopoeic origins and the notion of cosmological order. As we have seen, according to the former notion, the universe or portions of it, and all significant events, were created at the very beginning of time. They have a primordial character. They come ready-made from earliest times. The concept of cosmological order—a profound and basic idea in the Mesopotamian world view—assumed that all earthly and human manifestations were simply copies of divine models. For example, the Tigris and Euphrates rivers which existed on earth had their heavenly counterparts. Indeed, the heavenly rivers were more real than their earthly copies. To the Mesopotamian, the primordial models had existed since the very beginning of time, and all history consisted of an eternal return to the beginnings of things. Similarly, the primordial spatial models are cosmic in nature, and the specific earthly forms are mere representations of them. The earth and its representations are but a mirror of cosmic archetypes.

To the Sumerians, city-states were sacred entities. Each city belonged to its main god. Moreover, each had been assigned to its god on the day the world was created. Each city-state was thus linked by the Sumerians with the great primordial cosmic event—the creation of the world. Each city-state had accordingly been created full-blown at the time of the creation of the world, and it continued forever to influence human destinies. Besides, the Sumerian regarded each city-state as a copy or example of the universe, an instance of cosmic order in miniature. Each city-state was a microcosm of the macrocosmic universe: the processes at work in the universe were at work in the city.

The god of each Sumerian city-state owned it for all eternity. The water god, Enki, owned the city-state of Eridu forever, for he had been assigned it at the time of creation. The storm god, Enlil, was the possessor of Nippur, and the moon god, Nannar, was the proud owner of Ur, to cite further examples.

In recognition of the chief god and his sacred significance, the heart of each Sumerian city-state consisted of a temple complex or temenos—the most sacred precinct—which covered many acres. It contained the city's outstanding edifice—a great stepped tower called a ziggurat—plus a host of lesser temples and other buildings.

Ziggurats varied as to construction and size. In its fully developed stages, the ziggurat was generally a stepped tower of from three to seven stages, perhaps about one hundred yards square and sometimes attaining a height of one hundred fifty feet. At its top was situated a temple, while another temple was found at the foot. The ziggurat was usually dedicated to the god who owned the city for all eternity.

A creation of the Sumerians, the ziggurat became an outstanding permanent feature of all subsequent ancient Mesopotamian civilization. Not only Sumerians, but also Akkadians, Kassites, Babylonians, and Assyrians regarded it as the central monument of their religious worship. Indeed, as late as the third century B.C., under the Hellenistic Seleucid kings, a great ziggurat was constructed at Uruk in Mesopotamia in precisely the same style that had been employed almost two thousand years earlier—a testament to the remarkable persistence of an archaic sacred tradition. Even the Hebrews were indirectly influenced by the ziggurat with their notion of the Tower of Babel. The biblical Tower of Babel was undoubtedly the great ziggurat of the Marduk temple in Babylon, Etemenanki, which was made up of six square stages, one on top of the other, the last stage crowned by a chapel for the god.

Like the pyramid, the ziggurat has been a subject of a variety of interpretations by scholars. The most acceptable view is that it served as a kind of cosmic mountain. Many ziggurats of the Sumerian city-states had names which stood for a mountain; for example, the one at Nippur was designated "House of the Mountain, Mountain of the Storm, Bond between Heaven and Earth." The term mountain in Mesopotamia always designated a sacred mountain, the bond and meeting place between heaven and earth, a cosmic mountain located at the center of the world. The ziggurat was thus possibly a sacred representation in the cosmological order of the universe.

The temple complex was the spiritual dynamo, the energizing nucleus, the main center and focal point of the entire city-state. In a temple, it housed the dwelling place of the main god. In addition, there were a host of dwelling places for priests and priestesses who assisted the main god and lesser gods. Many rooms housed equipment employed by the cult in its elaborate acts of worship, including musical instruments, garments, and tools. The library, school, workshops, and granaries were also located within the temple complex, as was a great courtyard where the people could assemble on sacred festival days and bring their sacrificial and other offerings to the gods.

The god of the city was represented by a carved statue. But before he was placed in the inner sanctuary or cella of the temple, an elaborate sacred drama had to be performed. At Babylon the statue was carved of wood and lavishly decorated with fine stones and metals. In magical ceremonies, which took place in the workshop, at the river banks in a great torchlight procession, and finally in the cella, the statue received some fourteen washings of the mouth and an opening of the eye, designed to breathe life into it. Finally, the idol was introduced into the cella. Through magic, idol and god, symbol and reality, were now coalesced, and the "living" god in the form of the statue could henceforth perform his civic duties.

In theory, the entire city belonged to the main god. But in practice, the god and his priests—the temple organization—owned only a portion of the land which was worked directly for the god's benefit. If the city-state of

Lagash is exemplary, other fields were rented out each year by the temple organization to individuals, while a third class of fields was given to individuals rent free on a permanent basis in lots of various sizes. The Mesopotamian city thus provided for areas of private individual initiative. Although wealthy and powerful families owned large estates, many of the poor people possessed a garden and farm, a house and cattle.

Physically, the typical Sumerian city-state and many of the later Mesopotamian cities consisted of three parts. There was first of all the city proper, usually a walled area containing the temple complex and the palace of the king, together with the places of residence of the king's officials and the dwelling places of the citizens. Then there was the suburb or what the Sumerians called the "outer city," made up of farms, gardens, fields, and cattle folds. The "outer city" provided the inner city with food and raw materials. Thirdly, there was the harbor section called the *kar* by the Sumerians and *kāru* in Akkadian. This area functioned not only as a harbor but as the center of commercial activity, particularly with respect to overland trade. Various foreign traders lived and had their stores in the *kāru*, which had a distinct legal status and an administrative autonomy that protected those citizens who had business dealings in this area.

In the Sumerian city-state, which became the prototype of all subsequent Mesopotamian cities, three organizations were symbiotically interrelated and yet distinct —the temple organization, the community of free citizens, and the palace. The majority of inhabitants were free citizens enjoying economic, legal, and political privileges. In economic matters most of them were farmers, fishermen, cattle breeders, brewers, scribes, merchants, architects, doctors, or skilled artisans and craftsmen such as jewelers, potters, carpenters, masons, and smiths. The Sumerian city-state already witnessed a significant division of labor.

Artisans and craftsmen were able to sell their products in a free town market where they were paid either in kind or in money. Money took the form of silver ingots or rings that had to be weighed after each transfer. The practice of using silver as a standard, initiated by the Sumerians, continued throughout the entire period of Mesopotamian civilization, with two brief exceptions, once again illustrating the pervasive impact of the Sumerians.

The Mesopotamian economy was mainly agricultural, supplemented by trade in hair, leather, and wool. Apart from individual handicrafts, industrial production revolved around the weaving of textiles done in the workshops of the temple and palace. Trade between cities and surrounding countries was conducted by travelling merchants, and by both private individuals and by temple and palace representatives.

Slavery already existed as an institution in Sumerian times, but it was never extensive. The temples, the palace, and rich landowners had slaves. Those were normally prisoners of war and debtors, but there was a regular slave trade as well. The Sumerians allowed parents to sell their children in times of need. Foreign slaves, especially slave girls, were imported for their skills. Slaves were usually well treated, although there were apparently no specific laws among the Mesopotamians to protect them from harsh treatment. Injury to slaves required compensation to the master. There were also provisions for their manumission. Fundamentally, the master-slave relationship among the Mesopotamians had its cosmological analogue in the god-man relationship. Just as men were regarded as obedient slaves of their masters, the gods, so too were slaves to be the obedient servants of their earthly masters. In both instances obedience and subservience were regarded as prime virtues.

In very early Mesopotamian civilization, during the protoliterate period of the Sumerians, political power was apparently in the hands of the free citizens. There was a city governor called the *ensi*, but the citizenry exercised considerable power. The great expert on Mesopotamia, Thorkild Jacobsen, argued that this form of government constituted a primitive democracy, with the ultimate sovereignty in each city-state being vested in an assembly of all the adult freemen.[2] Every citizen could speak in the assembly, and the final verdict of the assembly was announced by a small group of lawmakers.

Characteristically, the Sumerians provided a cosmological basis for such primitive democracy in their mythology. Sumerian myths depicted the cosmos as a state. All of the gods came together in an assembly where they drank and made merry. They then discussed various issues broached by the senior gods. Each issue was open for general discussion among the gods, and any of the deities could speak his mind. After ascertaining the general will of the assembly, a decision was formulated by the senior gods and finally submitted to the whole assembly for approval.

In the early dynastic period of the Sumerians a most significant change took place. This was the rise of kingship and the institution of the palace. Modern historians trace this development mainly to the occurrence

---

[2] Other experts have denied that this was a democracy. William Albright, for example, considers it a gerontocracy, that is, a rule by elders.

of emergency situations within the city-state. As a result of more severe struggles between the city-states, increasing pressures from barbarian peoples, together with special problems of irrigation, leadership became a pressing necessity. The result was the election by the Sumerians in their assemblies of a king, or *lugal*, meaning "great man." As first, the king exercised temporary powers, but gradually kingship became a permanent hereditary institution.

The Sumerian kings established and led the army, which was based on the chariot and heavy-armored infantry in phalanx formation. The power of the Sumerian kings grew steadily and centered around the palace. In due course the palace competed with the temple as a center of wealth, influence, and power.

The ancient Mesopotamian would never have understood this secular account of the origins of kingship. Instead, in accord with the presuppositions of his world view, he interpreted kingship in origin and nature as having divine cosmological sanctions. Kingship for the Mesopotamians first existed primordially in the heavenly cosmos and then attained an earthly counterpart. Thus, in the *Sumerian King List*, which dates from the second millennium but includes traditions going back to the third millennium, specific reference is made to kingship as being lowered from heaven and initially instituted in the city-state of Eridu. The Sumerians had a tradition of a great flood which had swept away five of their cities. Significantly enough, after the flood it was necessary to reconstitute kingship on earth. Therefore, once again, the *Sumerian King List* speaks of kingship as being lowered from the heavens, with kingly dynasties now established in the city-states of Kish and Erech.

Four aspects of Mesopotamian kingship are of the

highest importance. These are kingship as a mandate from the gods, kingship as a linkage with the gods, kingship as the expression of the limited power of the gods, and kingship as an expression of the primordial world order. These four notions rest on the principle of cosmological order, namely that if the cosmos is a state, earthly government is but a replica or duplicate of the cosmic state.

Kingship in Mesopotamia was a mandate from the gods. The king was typically not himself a god but a *representative* of the gods. The Sumerian king acted on behalf of the god of the city and was thus usually a priest-king. Moreover, since the king was responsible to the cosmic gods for his every action, his authority was *delegated* to him from the rulers of the cosmos. In the Sumerian city-states the line between the *lugal* (king) and the *en* (high priest) was not clearly defined, since both claimed to be leading representatives of the gods.

However, the line between divine sanctions and divinity in kingship was at times obscured. Thus, while the Sumerian kings did not typically think of themselves as gods, from the time of Sargon of Akkad until Hammurabi, the name of the king was frequently written with the grammatical determinative *Dingir,* a term usually employed only with reference to gods or their worship. A certain divinization of kingship thus seems to have occurred during this period. With Hammurabi, however, the notion of the king as representative of the gods reasserted itself. By the time of the Assyrians, the king was regarded as the high priest of the god Ashur, that is, he was clearly only a representative, not an incarnation, of the gods.

As early as the Sumerians, the Mesopotamian king was linked with the divine ritual. During the great New

Year celebration, the final ceremony witnessed a royal holy marriage, a *hieros gamos*. This ceremony consisted of a sacred union between the ruling monarch and the goddess Inanna, who was the archetype of love, sex, and reproduction. The marriage was intended to ensure both the fertility of the soil and the fecundity of the womb. The ritual identified the king with the god of vegetation, Dumuzi, or, as the Bible calls him, Tammuz, the husband of Inanna. The eminent Sumerologist, Samuel Kramer, has demonstrated that Dumuzi was not the prototype of the dying and resurrected god, as was once generally assumed. Instead, Dumuzi dies in the Nether World and does not return. The king is Inanna's substitute for the dying Dumuzi. Since Inanna was the goddess of the city-state of Erech, in the annual marriage the king consummated the marriage by having sexual intercourse with one of the priestesses from the sacred temple at Erech, who was magically identified with Inanna. The annual ceremony was symbolic of the regenerative powers of the cosmos. The king, by participation, magically shared and enhanced the powers of nature and the cosmos.

Mesopotamian kingship was also an expression of the limited power of the gods. This notion will become more comprehensible if we take a closer look at the Mesopotamian view both of the universe and of their gods. In the Mesopotamian outlook, many things in the universe were alive. Generally, no distinction was made between the inanimate and the animate. The animate included not only familiar substances like salt, to whom the Mesopotamian addressed a personal appeal, but the earth, stars, stones, and, indeed, even abstract concepts. Everything in the universe had two aspects: one, a will or activating, dynamistic power called by the Sumerians *me*, and the other an essence, destiny or character, known as *nam*. There thus occurred among the Mesopotamians what some historians have called an anthropomorphization of the cosmos. Since everything possessed both a will and a character or essence, a *me* and a *nam*, the elements of the universe bore a resemblance to man, who also had a will and a character. The universe, or cosmos, was accordingly most appropriately represented as a vast assembly of gods in human form, an assembly of divine wills.

But in accordance with the principle of cosmological order, the Mesopotamian would never have conceded that his picture of cosmic society was founded upon and constituted an imitation of human society. Quite the reverse. To the Mesopotamian, human society was a copy of the primordial pattern of cosmic society. The gods took complete precedence over men, and any notion that men had created the gods in their own image would have been intolerable.

In this society of gods, in the assembly of the deities, there were distinctions of rank and importance. The leaders of the cosmic state were three gods who represented three basic elements in the universe. The most important god was Anu, the god of the sky. The sky spatially dominated the universe visible to the eye of the Mesopotamian and thus assumed a preponderant significance. The sky constituted the great "thou." Anu was the chief leader of the cosmic society of gods; his essence was authority and he was responsible for integrating the will of the other gods of the assembly to form final decisions.

Since Anu was both the essence and dynamism of authority, all other forms of authority in the universe partook of the *nam* and *me* of Anu. This was true of the father in his family and also of the Mesopotamian king. Anu was thus the primordial archetype of all fathers and the true prototype of all rulers. He held in his hands the original insignia of royal kingship consisting of the crown, scepter, shepherd's staff, and headband. These insignia had existed in heaven prior to any earthly kings as a possession of Anu. From heaven the insignia had come down to earth. Anu it was who thus called the Mesopotamian king into office. The king's commands were Anu's commands and required the same unquestioning obedience as direct commands from the great sky god himself. Moreover, everything else in the universe was subject to the *nam* and *me* of Anu and obeyed his orders as part and parcel of the laws of the cosmos.

The second leader of the cosmic assembly of gods was Enlil, the son of Anu. Enlil was lord in the region between heaven and earth, that is, the air. As such, he was in charge of the wind and an expression of the power of the storm. He was the embodiment of legitimate force. Enlil became the cosmic symbol of the growth and extension of the Mesopotamian state from a group of separate city-states to a more unified territorial state. In an inscription of the time of king Lugalzaggisi (ca. 2400 B.C.), who had embarked upon a policy that finally brought the whole of Sumer under his control, with Erech as his capital, the cosmic symbolism of Enlil as the territorial god was clearly illustrated. Enlil was called "king of all countries" and it was he who gave the kingship of the land to Lugalzaggisi. Enlil "laid all countries at his feet" and thereby combined the power of a god of legitimate force and a territorial god. The preamble to the Code of Hammurabi provided an even more elaborate description of Enlil's function as a cosmic symbol of territorial unity.

Enlil was called "lord of heaven and earth, who determines the destinies of the land . . ." and reference was
made to his lordship over all the people. In addition, a
parallel was drawn between the initial creation of order
in the form of an everlasting kingdom, Babylon, in heaven
under Marduk, and the establishment of the earthly
counterpart, Babylon, under the rule of Hammurabi. Here
was a vivid example of the Mesopotamian principle of
cosmological reproduction.

While Enlil exercised a lordship over the other city
gods from his sacred temple at Nippur, a third god, Enki,
completed the cosmic trinity of leading gods. In true
mythopoeic fashion, this god had multiple functions,
names, and characteristics. Indeed, Kramer has maintained that Enki was not a single god but two gods. As a
representation of the fertility of the earth, Enki was originally known as Ki. Here the god functioned as a female.
As Ki, the spouse of Anu, she was regarded as the mother
of all the gods. Another name for her was Nintu, which
means "the lady who gave birth." As Nenhursag she was
the great mother-goddess, the source of the earth's fertility.
As Ninmah she was the exalted lady or queen. She was
also known as the lady who determines fates, and the lady
who makes decisions regarding all heaven and earth.

But Enki was also male. Here he functioned as lord
of the earth, an embodiment of water. Water, with its
constant activity, represented the principle of creativity and
productivity. Enki, who was a minister appointed by Anu
and Enlil, was the god of the Mesopotamian craftsmen,
an overseer of rivers, canals, and irrigation, a source of
power for the priests' spells which protected men from
evil demons.

A second group of gods in the Mesopotamian

pantheon consisted of astral deities. These constituted a trinity representing the sun, the moon, and the planet Venus. The god of the sun was called Utu in Sumerian and Shamash in Semitic. The Mesopotamians regarded the sun god as the god of justice who had handed down the laws pertaining to human society. In the bas-relief of the Code of Hammurabi, Shamash is shown giving the laws to Hammurabi.

The moon god was called Nanna in Sumerian and Sin in Semitic. Great importance was attached to this god by the Mesopotamians, since the moon god controlled the night, the month, and the lunar calendar. He played a leading role in the vast omen literature of the Mesopotamians and in later Mesopotamian civilization was an important element in astrological and divination practices.

Reference has already been made to the third astral deity, the goddess Inanna, known as Ishtar in Semitic. She was already important among the Sumerians but attained tremendous significance after the Semitic conquests. She gradually came to supplant other female goddesses, so that the term Ishtar came to mean "the goddess." She revealed herself to the Mesopotamian as the Morning Star and the Evening Star—in short, as the planet Venus. Yet she was also, mythopoeically, at once a goddess of the earth, sex, love, and generation. Ironically, she was also a goddess of war.

These six gods, plus the lesser deities, formed the pantheon and constituted the assembly of the gods. The gods were different from men in two respects; they had immortality and they had divine powers. Yet occasionally Mesopotamian gods also suffered death. In the Babylonian Epic of Creation, Kingu, the consort of Tiamat, was slain by Marduk, who used his blood for the creation of man. In virtually all other respects, the Mesopotamian gods resembled humans. They had human forms, mated, produced families, dressed and ate like humans except that they had better clothing and choicer food, and experienced the gamut of human passions, especially love and hate. In addition to patterning their relations to one another on a familiar basis—father, mother, brother, and sister—they also mirrored the social fabric of the cities, using ministers, messengers, warriors, and slaves in the same way that their human counterparts did.

A most important characteristic of the Mesopotamian gods was that none of them was all-powerful or all-embracing. Even Anu who had enormous authority was not omnipotent. In this respect the Mesopotamian gods differed from the God of the Hebrews who was omnipotent, omniscient, and also uncreated. All of the Mesopotamian gods had been created, so that none of them had complete control or power over the universe. The assembly of the gods was really a locus and source of numerous powers. Because no one of the gods could predict what the will of the collective assembly would be at any one time, there was an arbitrary element in the decisions of the gods. This created an aura of uncertainty about their decisions. And since life on earth was for the Mesopotamian a replica of the cosmos, then this earthly life also had a basic element of insecurity. Moreover, since the gods were limited in their powers, the Mesopotamian king, as a representative of the gods, was also limited in his power. Kingship in Mesopotamia generally lacked the certainty, confidence, and absolutism that distinguished it in Egypt.

What was the position and role of man in this Mesopotamian picture of the cosmos? In general, the

Mesopotamians carried no very confident, secure, or high estimate of man. To the Sumerians, man had been fashioned of mere clay and he had been created for one purpose alone—to serve the gods. He was required to provide the gods with sufficient food, drink, and shelter, so that the deities would have leisure for their multifarious activities. He was completely subservient to the gods, catering to them in much the way a slave caters to his master. Moreover, the Sumerians were convinced that human life was suffused with uncertainty and anxiety; no one knew what destiny had been decreed for him by the arbitrary decisions of the gods. The whole of Mesopotamian civilization through its long span was dominated by this notion of the relative insignificance of man in the face of the gods, and by an abiding sense of insecurity.

Mesopotamian man sought, however, to take a number of measures to alleviate his anxiety and insecurity, though these were never entirely successful. One area of insecurity was that pertaining to relations between man and man. The Mesopotamian met this problem by honoring codes of law which he believed had been handed down by the cosmic gods to earthly kings to regularize property and social relationships. Ancient Mesopotamia had a high respect for the rule of law, demonstrated by the thousands of clay tablets written in cuneiform, the vast majority pertaining to legal matters, especially contracts.

The most famous of these codes was the celebrated Code of Hammurabi (ca. 1792–1750 B.C.), but it was both preceded and succeeded by other significant codes. Archaeologists have, for example, uncovered a portion of the Sumerian legal Code of Ur-Nammu (ca. 2113–2096 B.C.), which was inscribed on light-brown sun-baked bricks.

Three hundred years before the time of Hammurabi's Code, the *Lex Talionis* principle of an eye for an eye had already been modified among the Sumerians. The Code of Ur-Nammu provided for the payment of a sum of silver instead of retaliation for an offense in kind.

The Code of Hammurabi contained a prologue, giving the titles of Hammurabi and an account of his previous achievements. Then followed the code itself listing a wide variety of laws in areas such as the administration of justice, offenses against property, land and houses, merchants and agents, women, marriage, family property and inheritance, professional fees and responsibilities, agriculture, rates of hire, and ownership and sale of slaves. The code was followed by an epilogue which, among other things, described the purpose of the laws, and called upon succeeding rulers to follow in the path that Hammurabi had proclaimed in the Code.

Law codes like Hammurabi's were the literary expression of the kingly achievement in administration. Actual law consisted of royal proclamations (designed to correct specific abuses) and decisions based on custom or tradition. The law codes reflect an editing of the proclamations of a king's reign. They were no doubt designed to bolster the social fabric, and therefore often modified previous laws whenever this was deemed necessary. The Code of Hammurabi emphasized the principle of retaliation (*Lex Talionis*) more than some earlier law codes.

Another source of insecurity for Mesopotamian man was the world of demons. These were live evil spirits who infested the universe and threatened man at every stage of his life. Demons were ready to pounce upon people in lonely places, while they were asleep, during meals, and in childbirth. Demons could even attack the cosmic gods, and the Mesopotamians regarded the eclipse of the moon as an instance where the moon god, Sin, had temporarily been seized by a demon. The official and popular religion provided means for dealing with these demons. These included the wearing of amulets to ward off evil spirits and act as a prophylactic. If the individual were already possessed by a demon, magicians were called in. They were priests who were exorcists called *ashipu* and *mashmasu*. They frequently invoked the name of the Babylonian god of magic, Ea, father of Marduk. In a variety of ways, the magicians sought to drive the demons out of the body of the possessed—by incantations, symbolic or sympathetic magic, substitution magic, or the use of fire to burn out the evil spirits.

Still another realm of insecurity and anxiety was rooted, as we have seen, in the Mesopotamian's uncertainty regarding the destiny decreed for him by the arbitrary decisions of the gods. But here, too, Mesopotamian man was not entirely without recourse. Since the cosmic events and intentions of the gods were also reflected in their earthly counterparts, various techniques were available for overcoming this uncertainty. In the course of Mesopotamian civilization three great pseudosciences were evolved to fathom the destiny decreed man by the gods. One might use such special techniques as liver divination or hepatoscopy, which already flourished at the time of Hammurabi. A second technique was to search for omens in such phenomena as dreams, the behavior and movement of animals, or freakish births. An extensive omen literature and practice prevailed, resting on the assumption that if man discovered what misfortune was to befall him, he could avert it by the proper ritual. A third technique was astrology. Judicial astrology—the attempt to find out from a study of celestial and astrological phenomena what the near future held in store for both the king and the country in regard to floods, invasions, and harvests—may perhaps be traced back to the times of Sargon of Akkad (ca. 2371 B.C.). But horoscopic astrology—the view that any single person's future and fortunes are tied up to the positions of the heavenly bodies at the time of his birth—was a much later development in Mesopotamian civilization and had to await the invention of the zodiac.

One other recourse was open to man in his efforts to influence the decision of the gods and to seek their aid. He could throw himself on their mercy by means of prayer. Yet it was difficult for the individual Mesopotamian to pray directly to the powerful cosmic gods for, with few exceptions, these gods held themselves aloof from man. The Babylonian Epic of Creation quotes Marduk, the creator of man, as referring to "savage man." Therefore, in addition to the great cosmic deities, each Mesopotamian also called upon a personal god, who served as a protective genius and who probably was housed in a small chapel in his home. The Mesopotamian prayed to this protective god, asking him to intercede on his behalf in the assembly of the gods and to protect him from sickness and evil. Only when such an appeal failed did he dare approach the great gods.

Finally, the uncertainty and anxiety of the Mesopotamian extended even to the afterlife. True, death for the Mesopotamian was not equivalent to total annihilation. From the time of the Sumerians to the end of Mesopotamian civilization, the belief prevailed that in death the individual continued to maintain some form of existence which required nourishment, tools, utensils, and ornaments such as were needed in life. Yet what an afterlife! The

Mesopotamian believed that when a person died he continued a dreary, dismal, wretched existence in a lower world. To the Mesopotamian the dead were gathered in a giant, dark, forbidding, subterranean cave ruled by the goddess of the lower world, Ereshkigal, and her husband, Nergal. In the Epic of Gilgamesh, the great Mesopotamian literary masterpiece, Enkidu, the companion of Gilgamesh, refers to the lower world as a house of dust. Moreover, death wrought a change for the worse in the person. Man in the afterlife was but an empty shadow of his former self. Besides, the dead one perpetually threatened to return as a ghost, imbuing the living with terror and the perpetual threat of reprisal.

The Mesopotamian was convinced that he would never achieve true immortality, that death, in the form of a miserable, shadowy existence, was man's inevitable future lot. The fate of man was sealed at creation. This is the archaic mythopoeic message of the Epic of Gilgamesh and also of the Babylonian Epic of Creation. This man of clay must forever serve the gods in a world beset by uncertainty and travail.

EGYPTIAN

CIVILIZATION

The civilization of ancient Egypt lasted for almost three thousand years, from about 3200 B.C. to 332 B.C. Following the practice initiated by the Egyptian historian, Manetho, who flourished during the third century before the birth of Christ, the history of ancient Egypt is traditionally divided into thirty dynasties. The First Dynasty began with the unification of Egypt and the invention of writing; the last, or Thirtieth Dynasty, ended with the conquest of Egypt by Alexander the Great.

The problem of ancient Egyptian civilization is that of determining the relative importance of constancy and change. Inevitably, within such a lengthy period of time, numerous changes in politics, art, religion, economic life, and society took place. To highlight some of these, modern historians have created their own periodizations. For example, to designate the more important political developments, they speak of an Old Kingdom, also called the Pyramid Age, which extended from the Third through the Sixth Dynasties (ca. 2700–2200 B.C.); a Middle Kingdom centering in the Twelfth Dynasty (ca. 2000–1800 B.C); and a New Kingdom or Egyptian Empire, which lasted from the Eighteenth through the Twentieth Dynasties (ca. 1570–1090 B.C.). In addition, the Empire was succeeded by the periods designated as the Ethiopian Period (715–663 B.C.), the Saitic Revival during the Twenty-sixth Dynasty (663–525 B.C.), and the Persian Period (525–332 B.C.).

In spite of these modifications, ancient Egyptian civilization displayed a remarkable continuity, permanence, and identity. For example, it retained its basic mythopoeic pattern to the end. Apart from occasional lapses, the pharaoh, as god-king, played a central unifying role throughout Egypt's independent history. Again, the Egyptians, even during their great imperial adventures in the New Kingdom, never truly lost sight of their archaic beginnings and the foundations of their civilization. Indeed, the ancient Egyptian seems to have been quite unimpressed by the phenomena of change. To him the outstanding feature of the universe was its static character, its changelessness.[1] The cosmos, man, society, and the world of events were simply manifestations of fixed and recurrent patterns. Every aspect of the Egyptian's life was influenced by this fundamental characteristic of his world view.

The historian who wishes to do justice to ancient Egyptian civilization, both with regard to the way the Egyptians themselves mythopoeically viewed it and in respect to the manner in which the civilization unfolded historically, must take into account the joint factors of change and constancy which operated in this remarkable civilization.

---

[1] The doyen of Egyptologists, Pierre Montet, in his recent book *Eternal Egypt* (New American Library, 1964) insisted that "Egypt was a land of tradition where the same things went on recurring indefinitely. The Egyptians very rightly maintained that there had been no change since 'the time of the god.'"

The Thinite Period

The prologue to the first great act in the drama of Egyptian history—the Old Kingdom—took place during the first two dynasties, and is frequently designated as the Thinite Period. Named after the early city of This (or Thinis), located in Upper Egypt near Abydos, the Thinite Period was of vital importance in the formative phases of Egyptian Pharaonic civilization. One of the major achievements of this period was the development of hieroglyphic [2] writing, and significantly enough, the initial historical event that the Egyptians recorded was the unification of Upper (or southern) Egypt and Lower (or northern) Egypt under a single king. In Egyptian tradition this unification was ascribed to a ruler named Menes, although many modern Egyptologists believe it may have been the work of several kings, possibly Scorpion and Menes. The precise nature of the unification is still uncertain, but it appears that the creation of a united kingdom was accomplished by rulers from the south who subdued the northern kingdom of the Delta.

The phrase "the two lands" used by the Egyptians in recording their unification had historical, geographical, and cosmological significance. Throughout the independent history of ancient Egypt, tradition had it that Egypt was a double kingdom, a dual monarchy united under a

[2] This was a system of sacred characters (hieroglyphs) employed by the Egyptians both as ideograms (signs which represented objects and causes) and phonograms (signs that had a sound value). The idea of writing in Egypt may have been due to contacts with Mesopotamia, but the form of the writing was distinctly Egyptian.

single king. The kings had different titles in Upper and Lower Egypt. At the dawn of Egyptian history the kings on occasion wore a White Crown (Hedjet) which was the crown of Upper Egypt. At other times they wore the Red Crown, called Deshert, which represented Lower Egypt. During the Thinite Period a new Double Crown, called Sekhemti, was devised. It joined together the two crowns and persisted throughout the independent history of Egypt as the official crown of the king. Moreover, the kings maintained doubles of many of their government departments —one for Upper Egypt and one for Lower Egypt. For example, they had symbolically two treasuries but two actual sets of palaces. The elaborate ceremonial rituals for the king—his coronation, the Sed festival,[3] and his burial— were also duplicated in Upper and Lower Egypt with distinctive insignia and practices in each territory. One of the king's official titles was "King of Upper and King of Lower Egypt."

"The two lands" points up not only historical dualisms but geographic dualisms as well. From the standpoint of the outsider, Egypt appears as a geographic unity held together by the life-giving qualities of the Nile River. In that sense Egypt was "the land." But there were basic differences between the Delta and the valley, between Lower and Upper Egypt. The two lands gave expression to a geographic duality. The Nile River and the god-king might unite Lower and Upper Egypt, but the geographic differences between the Mediterranean-oriented Delta and the interior valley persisted and could not be erased.

To the ancient Egyptian, however, the root of this dualism was expressed not only in historical or geographi-

[3] See below, page 57.

cal factors but also in cosmological ones, since a basic principle of the cosmos was that totality resulted from an equilibrium of opposites. In the strife between two principles a static harmony and equilibrium is finally attained. Thus, the Egyptians saw the struggle between Upper and Lower Egypt as a strife between two gods, Horus and Seth, who were deadly enemies. In their struggles a higher total harmony was achieved, and embodied in the person of the king. Thus in some of the early Egyptian texts the king was appropriately called both Horus and Seth.

Egyptian Kingship

The nature of Egyptian kingship cannot be even remotely understood without taking into account its mythopoeic character. Its classic Egyptian definition was provided by a key official of the Pharaoh, the vizier Rekhmire, who lived in the New Kingdom during the Eighteenth Dynasty: "What is the king of Upper and Lower Egypt? He is a god by whose dealings one lives, the father and mother of all men, alone by himself, without an equal." The striking thing about this definition is that it is an excellent description of the way the Egyptians looked upon the king throughout their entire history. From the very first they regarded him as a god-king, a notion that never left them. Kingship to the Egyptian was not a human institution subject to the ordinary vicissitudes and fortunes of history. Instead, it was a divine institution, established at the moment of the creation of the world, which functioned ever after as part of the universal order. Kingship thus had cosmological sanctions and a divine function which manifested its eternality.

Our knowledge of the theoretical basis of Egyptian kingship depends heavily on a text called the "Memphite Theology." Though the only extant copy is a late one, there is every reason to believe that the Memphite Theology dates originally from the early dynasties. It expounded the religious teachings practiced at Memphis, which was regarded as the capital established by Menes. The theology linked the whole order of creation with the establishment by Menes of the unified land of Egypt. It thus made the act of Menes a part of a larger cosmological order of creation and rule.

The Memphite Theology elevated Ptah, who had originally been only the local god of Memphis, to a vastly more significant status. He was now represented as both the creator-god of the universe and the creator of the land of Egypt. As the creator-god of the universe, Ptah had created all the other gods, including the sun god Atum. The Egyptians possessed numerous accounts of creation, and many shrines in Egypt had creation mounds to designate the original place of creation. But the Memphite Theology did not hesitate to subordinate the most commonly revered creator-god, Atum, to Ptah. Indeed, all gods were looked upon as manifestations or emanations of the one god, Ptah. Moreover, Ptah created the universe because he first had a conception of it in his mind (or heart, as the Egyptians designated it). According to the myth, the universe came into existence when Ptah spoke with his tongue. He was thus a god of intelligence who actualized the preordained plan when he spoke. The Memphite Theology was notable for its emphasis on the unity of the divine and the oneness of the universe.

Unlike the God of the Hebrews, however, who was a transcendent God and stood outside of nature, Ptah, in mythopoeic fashion, was looked upon as the embodiment of an element of nature. The Memphite Theology referred to him as an earth god, who created cities and provinces, and who fashioned all the local gods and their cults down to the smallest detail. The various gods were pictured as entering into bodies made up of all kinds of wood, stone, or clay—in short, from material that is of the earth or Ptah himself. Thus, even the statues of the gods were embodiments of Ptah. Significantly, when Ptah had created "all things" and "all divine words," he was satisfied and he rested.

In addition to his role as creator of the universe, the Memphite Theology also designated Ptah as the "Lord of the Two Lands," thus indicating his close connection with Menes and the unification of Egypt. Memphis was called "the Great Throne," "the granary of the god," Ptah, because the temple of Ptah at Memphis provided sustenance to the two lands.

Ptah was linked with two important deities, Horus and Osiris. The living king was designated as the god Horus, while the king at his death became Osiris. The Egyptians considered the god Osiris to be buried at Memphis, but in mythopoeic fashion, each dead king was Osiris too. In this context, Horus and Osiris symbolized the royal succession from the dead king to the living successor. Horus the son embraced his dead father Osiris and, in a dramatic ritualistic mystery play, the myth of succession was re-enacted. At the accession of each king, the living king went through the ritual of burying his dead father in effigy. To the Egyptian, the living god Horus buried the dead god Osiris and assumed power. Kingship and royal succession were not only enacted on earth, but they were part of a re-enactment of a divine plan—the cosmic order of the gods.

If Egyptian kingship was the manifestation of a

preordained order destined to endure for all eternity, then any defection in practice from the principle of unified kingship was regarded less as a political failure than as a fundamental violation and sin against the cosmic order itself. In ancient Egypt there were a number of intervals when the unified power of the sacred kingship broke down. For example, during the first Intermediate Period (ca. 2200–2000 B.C.), following the Old Kingdom, a period of chaos and anarchy prevailed, with many nobles seizing independent power. The Twelfth Dynasty, which restored order after about 2000 B.C., regarded its task as the restitution of the preordained order established by the Lord of the Two Lands. This was equally true of the Eighteenth Dynasty, after ca. 1570 B.C., which threw out disruptive Asiatic invaders called the Hyksos; and of the Ethiopian or Twenty-fifth Dynasty (715–663 B.C.), which eliminated a number of minor dissident kings who had attempted power seizures. In each instance the aim was the same—to reconstitute the primordial order and to proclaim anew the initial historical event of Egypt, the unification of the two lands. The archaic foundations of Egyptian civilization were thus forever assured.

In mythopoeic thinking, names possess a magical significance, and a being does not need to have a single name because he does not have a single identity. Since the notion of unique identity is lacking, the same gods can manifest themselves in various forms, shapes, and manner with multiple names. As early as the Thinite Period of the first two dynasties, the kings had three of the five names that were later commonly employed during the Egyptian Empire. The person of the king was designated Horus, the great falcon sky god. This was his first and most important name. Secondly, the king also bore the name, "The

Two Ladies," symbolized by the vulture of the goddess Nekhbet of Upper Egypt and the cobra of the goddess Wadjet of Lower Egypt. Here the designation "The Two Ladies" represented the king's function as the unifier of the dual monarchy. Thirdly, the king bore a title, "He of the Sedge and the Bee," which is translated as "King of Upper and Lower Egypt," since the sedge, a coarse grasslike plant, stood for Upper Egypt, and the bee for Lower Egypt. In later times, during the New Kingdom, the king was also named "Horus of Gold," which indicated that the divine king, Horus, had an eternal, imperishable quality like gold and the glistening sun. Finally, the king was named "Son of Re," since the sun god, Re, also in time came to be regarded as creator and first king of Egypt. The term pharaoh was not used with reference to the king until the first millennium B.C. The word derives from the Egyptian *per-o*, meaning "great house," and was at first applied to the king's palace and then, by extension, to his person.

Whatever his titles, the Egyptian monarch functioned as a divine ruler with magical powers, a king blessed with charisma or special gifts and qualities, a being beyond the ken of mere mortals. His decisions for his people were the product of his divine power, creative depth and decision. But the Egyptian king, though a god, ought not to rule arbitrarily. Like all other things in the universe, he was subject to *Ma'at*.

Ma'at was a fundamental notion in the Egyptian world view and has been translated as "truth, justice, order." The Egyptians gave it various meanings and even a representation, but it always had reference to a fundamental reality in the universe. In mythopoeic fashion, *Ma'at* was pictured as the daughter of the sun god, Re, and

Egyptian statuettes reveal her as a diminutive, charming figure wearing an ostrich plume on her head. *Ma'at* was the incarnation of truth and justice. In the judgment that took place in the afterlife, the heart of the dead person was weighed against Truth, or *Ma'at*. The chief of all the courts of justice in Egypt—the vizier—regarded himself as the priest of *Ma'at*.

But *Ma'at* was more than truth or justice. It represented the cosmic principle of harmony, order, security, and equilibrium that had been initiated at the moment the demiurge created the universe and was reaffirmed each time a god-king came to secure the throne. The king, as the creator's successor, re-enacted *Ma'at* by once again putting order in place of chaos, truth in place of falsity, and instituting harmony instead of conflict. Nothing reveals the compelling power that *Ma'at* exercised over the Egyptian more than the statement of the Pharaoh, Amenhotep III (ca. 1398–1361 B.C.), that his whole aim as a ruler was to make the land of Egypt blossom as it had in "primeval times" by means of *Ma'at*. The universal order of the cosmos regulating its constituent parts, such as the movement of the heavenly bodies, the change of seasons, the daily rising and setting of the sun, the yearly inundation of the Nile, constituted a perfect order created after a preordained plan and eternally valid.

The concept of *Ma'at* provided the Egyptian with a sense of security, a confidence in eternality, and a trust in the king as the guardian of *Ma'at*. Security for the Egyptian in life as well as death, in social ethics and cosmic order, was assured through *Ma'at* from the moment of creation and reaffirmed forever after.

With kingship playing such a central role in Egyptian civilization, it was of the highest importance to preserve the health, potency, and vigor of the king. Already in the very early dynasties this was accomplished by means of the Sed festival. Its details are not wholly clear, but the festival seems to have functioned both as a commemoration of the king's accession to power and as an attempt to rejuvenate him. Celebrated every thirty years in later dynasties, it was performed more frequently in the early dynasties. The festival utilized priestly magic and other sacred rituals including one in which the king ran around a course called the "field" alternately dressed in the insignia of Upper and Lower Egypt. Four times he ran as king of Upper Egypt and four times as king of Lower Egypt. The "field" may have represented Egypt; as possessor of the land the king was assuring the prosperity and fruitfulness of his country.

The Old Kingdom

Two decisive achievements of the Thinite Period were, then, the idea of divine kingship and the concept of *Ma'at* which were interwoven in a mythological pattern by the ancient Egyptians. They provided one basis for a primary civilization that was to witness remarkable splendor and expansion in the next period, the Old Kingdom, or Pyramid Age which extended from the Third through the Sixth Dynasties (ca. 2700–2200 B.C.). The Old Kingdom was an age of great prosperity and achievement, an age whose most impressive symbols remain the great pyramids of the Fourth Dynasty (ca. 2650–2500 B.C.).

During the Old Kingdom, Egypt continued to be a theocracy in the literal meaning of that word—the rule of a state by a god. And one of the distinctive features of the Old Kingdom was the enormous increase in power and prestige of the kings. Egypt was a sacred state; to the Egyptians man, the gods, society, and nature were all part of a sacred universe. No distinction was made between the sacred and the secular and such a distinction would have been totally incomprehensible. Indeed, the Egyptian language lacked a word for state. The king was the state, since he was a god, and any word to designate authority apart from the king was unthinkable. True, the god-king was subject to *Ma'at*, but he was also the articulation and embodiment of *Ma'at*.

The Egyptian Bureaucracy

But what of officials, regulations, laws, and customs—in short, of bureaucracy and the codification of law? How were these viewed? The Egyptians never developed an impersonal concept of law which could become a permanent law code. There was nothing in Egypt to correspond to the Mesopotamian codes, and the reason is that in Egypt all law was viewed as the expression of the personal authority of the god-king. He governed by decrees which might actually conform to the customary law of the land, but which could just as well be arbitrary products of his personal will and whim.

Although the god-king was the state, he required assistance in governing the unified land of Egypt. In order to govern so large and complex a realm a bureaucracy was an obvious necessity. As early as the First Dynasty there were high officials invested with a cylinder seal as a sign of their function. But the way the system of administrative and bureaucratic functionaries operated was regarded by the god-king as a peculiarly personal matter. Since he was a magical and charismatic god-king, all authority had to be intimately related to him. That is why originally all high officials were related by blood to the king or the royal house. They were regarded as a distinct class—The Royal Kinsmen. They shared in the king's charisma, in his magical power, in his essence and mystery as a being apart from men and yet acting for the welfare of the whole land.

The transmission of the god-king's powers to his kinsmen could not remain on a completely personal level, however, and ultimately required the routinization of charisma—that is, the creation of established patterns for the diffusion of the extraordinary, divine powers of the king. In the first three dynasties, the king was directly in charge of the various branches of administration, but in the Fourth Dynasty, under the liberal and able king, Snefru (ca. 2700 B.C.), a new office was instituted called *tjaty*, or vizier. The vizier was in the beginning a prince of the royal household, but later he was chosen from among the scribes and trained at court. He was the chief of the bureaucracy and bore the titles "Steward of the Whole Land" and "Councilor of All Orders of the King." The office of vizier persisted until the fourth century B.C.

The vizier was responsible to the king, received instructions from him, and reported to his lord. The Egyptian texts speak of the vizier as being the will of the master and the eyes and ears of the sovereign. If the king were to place his trust in him, it was essential that the vizier be the wisest of the wise. Though there was an intimate personal relationship between the two, the routinization of charisma was exhibited in the vizier's role as chief of the bureaucracy. For example, in the wisdom literature of the vizier Ptahhotep, written during the Old Kingdom, the virtues that are especially praised are respect for custom and for the hierarchy, rather than the divine will of the king.

In its final form, the vizierate had control over a large administrative bureaucracy that included a number of departments—public works, treasury, agriculture, police, chancellery, judgment of appeals, and river transport. The vizier was minister of justice and on his chest hung a small figure of *Ma'at*, the goddess of the cosmic order. The vizier had messengers and agents travelling throughout Egypt and reporting to him. No transaction involving land could be completed without a registry in his office.

Land registry points up the vital role played by agriculture in Egyptian civilization. In the Old Kingdom, the two most important departments were those of the treasury and of agriculture, an indication of the intimate connection between wealth and land. The treasury department, known as the "Two White Houses," had branches throughout Egypt for the collection of taxes. Censuses were conducted of fields, gold, and cattle. The treasury department then as now invaded numerous areas of life and utilized an increasingly large and complex bureaucracy. The government had to be sure that its innumerable officials would have food in case of lean years which might produce famine.

The whole Egyptian economy was based on barter, and taxes were paid in kind. Each year the treasury department sent its agents, in the form of a commission, to measure the arable land, to compile a list of tenants and holders of the land (both corporate and individual), and to estimate the future output and the likely tax yield. Then, after the wheat and barley had started to grow, other treasury experts fixed the actual amount of the tax. These experts consisted of a legal scribe, two scribes from the land registry office, a representative of the overseer, a so-called keeper of the cord, and a stretcher of the cord.

The land of Egypt, in addition to being a double monarchy, was divided into nomes or provinces called *sepats*. In prehistoric Egypt, there had existed a number of independent tribes, each with its own standards in the form of gods such as the bull or cow. When Egypt became a united kingdom the old tribal standards became the emblems of the new administrative provinces or nomes. The head of each nome was an official called a nomarch.

In theory, the nomarchs were in charge of particular provinces but completely loyal to the king; indeed, they were his representatives in the provinces. Their task was to carry out the orders of the vizier and king in the provinces, to supervise a host of people who worked on the royal domains, to maintain police order and guard the frontiers, and to head the provincial administration. But by virtue of their extensive powers, the nomarchs constituted a potential source of danger to the centralized rule of the king. Moreover, they gradually acquired large land holdings and became a hereditary official class, increasing their power and prestige greatly. Thus by the end of the Old Kingdom the nomarchs became a countervailing force to the centralized bureaucratic system of the king, and contributed enormously to the anarchy and chaos of the succeeding First Intermediate Period.

We can see that Egyptian bureaucracy had already in practice moved a long way during the Old Kingdom. It had become highly routinized and complex, employing innumerable bureaucrats exemplified in the profession of the scribe, the bureaucrat par excellence. He was the master of writing. (In the Egyptian bureaucracy written records were everywhere.) He never tired of proclaiming his vital bureaucratic role. In many accounts written on papyri the scribes repeatedly boasted that they were the ones to impose and collect taxes, that it was they who kept an account of everything, that armies could not operate without them, that they set the pace for every man.

There is no doubt that the profession of scribe was considered sacred and honorable. In the Old Kingdom some of the royal princes reserved the right to have statues made of themselves as scribes, thus indicating the reverence they felt for the profession. The conceit of the scribes regarding their own role was largely attributable to the fact that most of the Egyptians were illiterate, and the scribe, as an educated man, could separate himself from ordinary people. He probably paid no taxes and was held in esteem; whether he used hieroglyphic inscriptions or the speedier hieratic cursive script, as a member of the literati he was performing a vital role in this sacred Egyptian civilization.

Two other features of the Egyptian bureaucracy are worth mentioning. One is that it eventually showed a considerable degree of social mobility, so that men from the lower ranks could rise to important positions. The king was always on the lookout for able men and once he spotted a potential talent, movement to a higher echelon could quickly follow. Yet one must always bear in mind, as the Egyptologist John A. Wilson has observed, that state and society in Egypt were hierarchical. At the very apex was the god-king who not only ruled Egypt but was the owner of the whole land and controlled the property and lives of his subjects. The king was above the vizier and the national ministers, as these were above the governors of the provinces or nomarchs, who in turn were superior to the mayors of the many small villages. In re-

ligion the king was supreme over the priests, who were
above the people. In society the king was above his nobles,
who were superior to the merchants and artisans, who
likewise were above the serfs. The realities of the situation
were that the king delegated functions to a ruling group
consisting of nobles, priests, scribes, and large landholders
who carried out the decrees of their god-king and acted
only in his name.

Beneath this ruling group were the common people,
many of whom were tillers of the soil. They were serfs who
were obligated to give part of their crops to the king in
the form of taxes. Their bodies belonged to the king, and
they were subject to military service and to the *corvée*,
or forced labor, exacted by the government for the construction of various public works such as dikes, canals,
temples, and pyramids. The king could also at his will
commandeer artisans and merchants for public works proj-
ects. The common people thus lacked real freedom even
though some, like the artisans, were given opportunities to
pick their jobs, and in theory all were protected by the
god-king's observance of *Ma'at*.

The Pyramids

Such, in brief, was the state and society which
flourished in ancient Egypt during the Old Kingdom and
which was typical of the whole of archaic Egypt. The
hierarchical structure of the society corresponded strikingly
to the most remarkable attainment in architecture during
the Old Kingdom—the great pyramids themselves. These
were indicative of the enormous power and prestige acquired by the kings of this period, of their unshakable

belief in the principle of eternality, and of an artistically triumphant fusion of geometric clarity and enigmatic mystery.

The great pyramids must not merely be regarded as isolated, self-sufficient, gigantic royal tombs distinguished by square bases and four equal triangular sides joining at an apex. Egyptian archaeologists have demonstrated that the great pyramids were the central focus of a vast funerary area which collectively resembled a city of the dead—a necropolis.

The funerary area consisted of a number of parts. One was the Valley Chapel located at the edge of the desert, a building stately and dignified though not large. A walled-in causeway, often more than a quarter of a mile long, led from the Valley Chapel to a Funerary Temple proper, which was always located on the east side of the pyramid. The Egyptians were convinced that the dead king would leave his tomb and partake of many fares and ceremonies including those in the funerary area, and for this reason, a false door, in imitation of a real doorway, was recessed on the east side of the pyramid adjoining the Funerary Temple. In close proximity to the great pyramid of the king, smaller pyramids were situated— the tombs of the king's wives and daughters. Nearby were a series of mastabas or oblong structures with flat roofs and sloping sides, which served as the tombs of princes, courtiers, and officials. The mastabas were laid out in neat rows that resembled orderly streets in a planned town, indicating once again that the vast funerary complex constituted a city of the dead. The use of pyramids as tombs was restricted to royalty during the Old Kingdom. All others—servants and worshippers—were confined to lesser tombs. On several sides of the pyramid were located full-sized boats placed in covered trenches, which pointed to all four directions of the compass. These boats probably were designed to enable the king to voyage wherever he desired in the afterlife just as he had in this life.

Scholars have attempted to trace the origin of the great pyramids back to practices beginning with the First Dynasty and even to predynastic Egypt. Such endeavors are based on the assumption that they were the product of several stages in the evolution of Egyptian mortuary practice. Common to all such practices was the firm Egyptian belief in a life after death. In predynastic Egypt a rectangular mound of sand was placed above the pit-graves. Such mounds were continued in the First Dynasty and are found, for example, in the brick mastabas at Sakkarah. They appear to have no architectural function.

In the late predynastic period and during the first dynasties, all the kings and nobles were buried in mastabas. These consisted of a substructure below the ground and a superstructure of brick built on top of the ground in the shape of an oblong rectangular platform. The use of brick was probably Mesopotamian in origin and influence, since the Egyptians had a plentiful supply of stone. The oblong superstructure of the mastaba was constructed in imitation of a dwelling house. Indeed, the Egyptian regarded the tomb as his house and provided it with all manner of domestic installations. In a number of tombs of the Second Dynasty lavatories were provided near the burial chamber, since death was but a continuation of life and life's needs had to be served even in death.

In the Third Dynasty, at the start of the Old Kingdom, a number of significant developments transpired. Under King Djoser, a remarkable architectural genius called Imhotep, emerged. He was responsible for design-

ing and constructing the great mortuary complex at Sakkarah which centered around a step pyramid, the first of
the Egyptian pyramids. It consisted of six enormous steps
on all four sides and rose to a height of about 200 feet.
Surrounding it was a great wall and within the enclosure
were altars, shrines, courts, storehouses, and tombs. In the
subterranean passages of the pyramid dwelt the *ka* of
King Djoser. The *ka* was the vital energy of the king, both
as a creative force and a sustainer of life. It represented
the divine creative power and the forces which gave
power to *Ma'at*. Djoser's *ka* could still issue orders, participate in the Sed festival, and sustain itself eternally.
Two tombs of King Djoser were contained within the
mortuary complex. One was located underneath the step
pyramid where Djoser's mummy was situated, while the
other was attached to the south enclosure wall.

Two other developments under Djoser were of first
importance. A distinction was now made between the
burial tombs of the king and those of the high nobles and
officials. Henceforth only the king and his immediate family were buried in pyramids. The nobles and officials were
buried in mastabas, a practice that continued for centuries.
Secondly, the step pyramid of Djoser was built entirely of
limestone, and this symbolized the triumph of stone over
brick. Brick was a relatively perishable material; stone was
eternal.

Under King Djoser's successors three more step
pyramids were constructed, but they were inferior to the
achievement of Imhotep. In the Fourth Dynasty under
King Snefru there were two new developments. A step
pyramid constructed at Meidum, some 33 miles south of
Sakkarah, was modified when the eight steps were filled
in to form a regular pyramid. And the practice was in-

stituted of having a Valley Chapel leading to a causeway which joined the Mortuary Temple on the east side of the pyramid. A smaller pyramid was also constructed for the queen on the south side. Thus, the basic pattern for the mortuary complex of the great pyramids was established. Under Snefru's son, Cheops, the largest of all the pyramids was constructed at Gizeh. This "great pyramid" covered an area of over 13 acres and rose to a height of 481.4 feet. Its four sides were oriented with remarkable precision on the four points of the compass. There was only one entrance, on the northern side, 55 feet about the ground.

The interior planning of Cheops' pyramid was modified three times. In the first attempt a tomb chamber was constructed underground and was abandoned. A second tomb chamber in the body of the pyramid was also abandoned. In the third attempt, an ascending corridor led from the entrance corridor into the heart of the pyramid. This corridor gave way to a Grand Gallery, which was 153 feet long and 28 feet high. This Grand Gallery was used only once, to carry the mummy of the king in his coffin to the funeral chamber. The chamber was constructed entirely of granite, and it contained the lidless sarcophagus of the king. Nine blocks of granite weighing about 400 tons made up the ceiling of the funerary chamber. Above it were some five separate compartments designed to reduce the pressure on the ceiling so that it would not collapse.

Once the funeral services were completed and the body of the king was placed in the sarcophagus within the funerary chamber, the chamber itself was sealed off with large slabs, and other blocks were also placed in the ascending corridor. A special shaft was hewn by the workmen leading to the first burial chamber, enabling them to leave the pyramid, but the first burial chamber was also blocked. In short, the pyramid was forever sealed off to humans.

The other two great pyramids at Gizeh—those of Chephren and Mycerinus—were also glorious architectural achievements. Chephren, the son of Cheops, emulated his father by constructing a second giant pyramid, but the pyramid of Mycerinus covered only half the area of the great pyramids. Later pyramids were of smaller size.

Although there was an evolution of Egyptian tomb architecture from the predynastic rectangular mounds of sand, to the mastabas, to the step pyramids, to the full pyramids, each of these forms of tomb architecture had a special symbolic significance. The leading authority on the pyramids, I. E. S. Edwards, has argued for the following interpretations. The rectangular mound of sand was regarded by the Egyptians as resembling the hill which had emerged from the primeval waters when the earth was created. It thus symbolized existence and functioned as a counter to death. The mastaba, which was a replica of the Egyptian's house, signified that the spirits of the dead would be properly housed. The step pyramid and the great pyramids developed under the impact of the rising sun-cult, whose center and priesthood were at Heliopolis, near the capital city of Memphis. Imhotep, the creator of the step pyramid, was a priest of Heliopolis. According to the myths of the sun-cult, the king would spend much of this afterlife with the sun god or else he himself would function as the sun god. In any case, it was necessary for the king to reach the solar region. Among the devices mentioned in the pyramid texts for reaching the solar region were two—the staircase and the rays of the sun. The step pyramid might thus be conceived to resemble a staircase to enable the king to reach the sun. As for the pyramid proper, it reproduced the appearance of the rays of the sun. Thus, by means of the pyramids the kings could ascend to the sky and then return to partake of the food placed daily by the priests in the Funerary Temple.

Egyptian Art

The pyramids exemplified a fundamental feature of Egyptian art—exploitation of the aesthetic possibilities of plane surfaces. All of Egyptian architecture, sculpture, and painting was based on the principle of the plane surface. The great pyramids of the Fourth Dynasty were artistic triumphs of the geometric use of plane surfaces, for the pyramid was a series of these surfaces arranged with a common apex. Egyptian sculpture in the round and in relief were likewise characterized by plane surfaces. The limbs of statues were extended or projected by the use of parallel upright planes. In the Egyptian relief sculptures, the supremacy of the plane was exhibited both in sunken relief and in surface relief. Always there was the feeling that the relief was part of the surface and that it never departed from the surface area.

In painting, the triumph of the plane surface was again evident. An Egyptian painting was a simultaneous series of plane surfaces presented as reality. The body and limbs were not depicted as they appeared at any particular moment in time—that is, from a particular space-time perspective. Instead, the essential reality of the different planes was stressed. The body was thus for the Egyptian not a series of momentary appearances to the eye, but a group of eternal structural planes. Thus the face was shown in profile as a plane; the eye was likewise depicted as a distinct plane, looking at the spectator; the bust was shown from the front as another plane. The hips were slightly turned, while the legs were shown from the side. The Egyptian penchant for such surfaces was manifested again in the desire of the artist to show both shoulders as essential plane surfaces. Even Egyptian writing in the form of hieroglyphics—a form of picture writing—appeared as a series of continuous horizontal or vertical planes undivided by words or punctuation signs, and lacking depth.

Egyptian painting established a hieratic style at the very beginning and maintained its basic conventions with few exceptions throughout Egyptian history. The intent of the painting in tombs, temples, and ritual objects was thoroughly mythopoeic. Since no real distinction was made between life and death and the dead one had to be provided with the things he had enjoyed in this life, the wall paintings on the mastabas of the Old Kingdom depicted the objects that the dead one would require in the afterlife. The paintings, in short, magically fulfilled the needs of the departed. The subjects represented were generally not morbid, since death was accepted optimistically —indeed was welcomed as a constitutive part of the eternal order of things. On numerous walls, scenes were depicted showing Egyptians plowing, harvesting, gathering flax, and fattening animals. Other scenes revealed scribes making a survey of cattle and grain. These wall scenes unquestionably functioned magically to provide ritualistic funeral offerings, by supplying the deceased with his nourishment, with his food and banquet needs.

The principle of eternal recurrence was central to the world view of the Egyptians, but the principle of linearity or a straightforward progression in time from beginning to end was lacking. Instead, the Egyptian thought in terms of cycles. We have seen that each king reaffirmed *Ma'at* when he came into office. That signified that he returned to the everlasting beginnings of the cosmic order and renewed it. Kingship was thus part of a pattern of eternal recurrence. Two other expressions may be noted. One was the daily recurrence of the sun and the other the annual recurrence of the overflow of the Nile. The sun god and the god Osiris were the respective gods of these vital cycles and both were interpreted mythopoeically by the Egyptians.

The Sun in Egyptian Religion

Let us take a closer look at the role the sun and the Nile played in Egyptian life and thought. The sun, by virtue of its brilliant light and great heat, would automatically inspire an attitude of awe and respect in a land such as Egypt. But since the sun was also the giver of life, the ripener of the crops sown by man, it naturally took on an overwhelming significance and came to be worshipped not only as a god but as a model god.

This worship of the sun as source of all life was promulgated above all by the priests of a sun cult located at Heliopolis, near Memphis, a few miles north of present-day Cairo. We have seen how certain mythopoeic notions associated with the Heliopolis sun cult were reflected in the form and structure of the pyramids. But the sun cult was not restricted to Heliopolis and its priests; it flourished throughout Egypt. Every significant local god was somehow associated or identified with the sun god and the ritual practices in many temples dedicated to other gods likewise came to be patterned after the Heliopolis sun temple.

In a mythopoeic view of the world, a god may possess many different names, shapes, and forms. The god can appear in a number of places and perform a number of different functions simultaneously. To the Egyptians and those who shared the presuppositions of a mythopoeic outlook, there appeared to be no inconsistency or contradiction in any of this. What appears to us as a blatant violation of logic was simply not subject to logical analysis by the Egyptians. The sun god accordingly had several names and forms. As Atum he had a completely human form and was represented as wearing the double crown of Egypt, the Red Crown of Lower Egypt and the White Crown of Upper Egypt.

The sun god was also represented in another form— Khepra, the sacred scarab beetle. The priests of Heliopolis believed that the rising sun came forth like the scarab from its own substance and was reborn of itself. There were no females of this species of beetles, only males, according to the Egyptians. They deposited their seed in small round pellets and rolled them along with the hind legs. The Egyptians believed this action mirrored the course of the sun from east to west.

In a third representation, the sun god had the name Re and assumed the form of a human body with the head of a falcon. Here the sun god was identified with Horus, another solar god. Re was crowned with the solar disc and the cobra. By the Fifth Dynasty in the Old Kingdom, Re was officially acknowledged as the head of the pantheon of gods. Every morning Re appeared at dawn from behind Manu, the mountain of sunrise, and sailed across the sky in his own solar boat accompanied by the gods of his retinue. The voyage across the sky was conceived mythopoeically as a dramatic ritual which used all three forms. At dawn the sun god was a child represented by Khepra; at noon he had become a full-grown man, Re; and at sunset he assumed the form of an old man, Atum, who disappeared into the western horizon. At night, in a second ship, he sailed through the underworld and emerged in the morning to repeat his daily journey. The myth gave remarkable concrete representation to the eternal daily recurrence of the sun.

The sun god was also identified with the creation of the world. In this version of the creation—one of a number—there existed at the beginning of time neither earth, sky gods, nor men. Only Atum was present in a great watery mass called Nun which filled the entire universe. In order to create other elements, Atum generated two other gods by spitting them out of his mouth. These were the god Shu (air) and the goddess Tefnut (moisture). Shu and Tefnut in turn, by their own union, produced two children, Geb, the earth god, and Nut, the goddess of the sky. From these came four children, Osiris and his consort Isis, and another couple, Seth and his consort Nephthys. These nine constituted the Great Ennead or the nine gods of Heliopolis and became the most important gods in the official Egyptian pantheon.

The first five gods of the Great Ennead were clearly cosmological deities engaged in the activity of generating the primordial elements. Thus Geb (earth) and Nut (sky) were locked in a tight embrace. But Shu (air) came between them and tore them apart. Shu (air) raised Nut (sky) upward to become the sky. Geb (earth) was left lying prostrate beneath her. The Egyptians pictured the sky god Nut as a colossal goddess; her feet touched the eastern horizon, while her body curved above the earth, and her arms hung down to the level of the setting sun.

The other four gods of the Great Ennead had no part in forming the universe but represented connections between the gods and men, especially in the institution of divine kingship. Thus, as we have seen, Osiris represented the dead king who is eternally succeeded by his own live son, Horus. Isis, who was both sister and wife of Osiris, stood for the throne of the god-king. Nephthys, though the wife of Seth, helped Isis to sustain Osiris. Seth represented the classical god of the opposition—he became the god of the desert as opposed to the fertile land, and the implacable opponent of Osiris. The Great Ennead, in summary, encompassed both the Egyptian order of creation and of society.

The sun god was also linked with the creation of mankind. In one account, the sun god described how he wept upon the limbs of his body, and from the tears man was formed. The Egyptian word for mankind was *remeth* and for tears, *remyt*. But having created man, the sun god resolved to remove him from the face of the earth because he was evil and rebellious. In a remarkable myth the Egyptians described how Re sent down his own eye in the form of the cow goddess, Hathor, who slaughtered much of mankind. Yet mankind was finally saved by a clever ruse. At Re's direction the deities prepared some 7000 vessels of a very powerful beer which was mixed with a red coloring matter to resemble blood, and then emptied on the face of the earth. Hathor drank from the mixture which covered the fields, became drunk, and was unable to recognize mankind.

Finally, the sun god was mythopoeically linked with

the king. As noted previously, the king came to be regarded as the physical son of the sun god. From the time
of Chephren (ca. 2620 B.C.) in the Old Kingdom the king
was designated "Son of Re." But the king was also the
earthly embodiment of Re. On the king's forehead was
the golden uraeus cobra, a special emblem of the sun god
which spat fire when the king fought in battle. After the
death of the king, he always joined his father in the sky,
where he reigned in glory as an aspect of the cycle of
eternal recurrence.

Osiris in Egyptian Religion

If the sun god was the exemplary embodiment of
the principle of creativity, the god Osiris came to be the
prime symbol of resurrection in Egyptian civilization. The
theme of the dying and resurrected god, as a manifestation of eternal recurrence, was given a rich and colorful
imagery and significance by the Egyptians. Osiris became
the composite syncretic representation of the theme of
death and resurrection in the realms of kingship, vegetation, the Nile flood, the heavenly bodies, and the afterlife.
In the popular religion of the Egyptians a great legendary
myth was created to symbolize this resurrective function
of Osiris. No Egyptian account of the legend has come
down to us complete, but we possess a Greek version
handed down by Plutarch, and there is every reason to
believe that it is reasonably authentic.

In the Egyptian calendar the year contained 365
days divided into twelve months of thirty days, plus five
additional or epagomenal days which came at the end of
the year. According to the legend, Osiris was born on the

first of the five epagomenal days and became king of the
world, that is, of Egypt. He was represented as bringing
civilization to the Egyptians, giving them laws, and teach-
ing them respect for the gods. His constructive, civilizing
role brought him into mortal opposition with his evil
brother Seth who formed a plot to destroy him and seize
the kingdom for himself. Seth collected seventy-two accomplices, secretly secured the measurements of Osiris'
body, and ordered a beautifully decorated coffer to be
made, to the exact measurements of Osiris. At a banquet,
Seth brought in the coffer and offered it to anyone who,
when lying in it, would fit it exactly. After the various accomplices made the attempt and failed, Osiris was per-
suaded to lie down inside. The accomplices then shut the
coffer lid, secured it with nails and molten lead, then
hurled it into the Nile where it eventually went out to sea.

Isis, Osiris' wife, then began a quest for his body.
In one Egyptian version, she found it dead on the shore
of Nedit near Abydos. In Plutarch's account, she found it
at Byblos, in Lebanon, and after a number of adventures
brought the chest back to Egypt and hid it. But Seth
found the hiding place, cut the body of Osiris into pieces,
and scattered them over the land of Egypt. Isis recovered
nearly all of the pieces and buried them.

Next came the resurrection of Osiris for which various accounts were provided. In one description it was
done by Anubis, the jackal-headed god, who carefully
embalmed the portions of Osiris according to instructions
from Re. The god Thoth and the mother of Osiris, Nut,
were also believed to have had a part in the resurrection.
The goddesses Isis and Nephthys were, in one dramatic
ritual, represented as flapping their great wings over the
head of Osiris in an effort to restore life to him. In every

version, magic or *hike* was employed to bring forth the powers latent in Osiris to resurrect himself.

Revenge for the death of Osiris now ensued. Isis conceived a son, Horus, from her dead husband, and the son became the avenger of the father, castrating Seth. Finally, the gods intervened in the struggle between Horus and Seth; the universe was divided between them, and there ended the great popular legend of the death and resurrection of Osiris.

In both popular religion and official cult, Osiris was also associated with the resurrective qualities of grain, symbolizing the vegetation which died at harvest but regularly reappeared. (However, the great harvest festival itself was not dedicated to the god Osiris but to a generative god named Min.) Similarly, Osiris was associated with the resurrective vitality of the soil and the Nile (again, despite a separate god for the river), and thus the water of the annual inundation, called "young water," was identified with his name. The annual rise of the Nile, coinciding with the Egyptian New Year, was a leading seasonal celebration, a manifestation of the resurrection of Osiris. In another celebration which took place when the waters had receded, the goddesses Isis and Nephthys were represented as bemoaning the fate of the dead Osiris. Thus did Osiris symbolize the vital cycles of the Egyptian land and its life-giving river.

Osiris was not only linked with kingship, the earth, vegetation, and the Nile in their resurrective functions; he was also connected with the heavenly bodies. As early as the pyramid texts Osiris was identified with the star constellation, Orion, and the star which was close by, Sothis, was identified as Isis. In a late Egyptian text Isis related how Orion (Osiris) rose and set each day and the star

Sothis (Isis) promised to follow and never desert him. Moreover, Osiris was also identified with the moon and its eternal alterations.

Finally, Osiris was King of the Dead, Lord of the Underworld; here he had an intensely personal message and significance for the Egyptian as the sympathetic god who suffered, died, and was resurrected. And in the god's resurrection, the Egyptian saw a way to overcome the grave and achieve his own resurrection.

A distinction must be made between means and ends in the Egyptian's perception of death, eternality, and the afterlife. From predynastic times, the Egyptian had believed that death did not mark the end of his existence, since death was a continuum of life. Therefore, the principle of eternality and the afterlife was accepted from the start as a basic postulate of Egyptian civilization. The real problem for the Egyptian was not the belief in an eternal life, but the means of assuring it.

As to techniques and means of achieving an afterlife, the Egyptians tried three different approaches. One centered on the notion that the grave or tomb, as the house of the Egyptian, would forever ensure another life. The dead one would experience within his tomb a renewed existence with the same needs and requirements as before. Hence, the elaborate care taken in funerary provisions. A second approach was developed during the Old Kingdom, at first among kings, then among courtiers, and, following the Old Kingdom, as an even wider concept of funerary practice. This approach centered upon the sun god Re. As a result of two rituals called the "tent of purification," and "solar lustration," the dead one could be taken to the paradise of the sun god where he was judged. The dead one was taken in the sun god's boat to eternity, where he forever accompanied the god on his eternal cycle of cosmic recurrence.

In addition to these, a third approach based on the Osirian notion of the afterlife gradually took on a more universal significance in succeeding periods. In mythopoeic fashion all three approaches to the afterlife continued to function among the Egyptians, but the Osirian assumed the leading role.

As a King of the Dead, Osiris was represented in human form. His body was covered with a white funeral wrapping, while in his hand he held the crook and the whip, symbols of kingship. His face and hands were colored green, like the vegetation of the earth. His crown was a white cap, the crown of Upper Egypt, with two feathers on either side, which represented *Ma'at*.

Osiris eventually presided as King of the Underworld in mythopoeic dramatic ritual, the Judgment of the Dead. In one corner of the Underworld was a Judgment Hall, also known as the Hall of Two Truths, where, after death, the departed ones were taken. There, in the presence of Osiris, Isis, Nephthys, the four sons of Horus, and the other great gods, the dead one was judged. Forty-two gods, representing the 42 nomes of Egypt, were also present as assessors.

In the presence of all these, the Egyptian made a negative confession, denying that he had committed 42 specific sins—for example, "I have not robbed," and "I have not been covetous." While this proceeded, two gods, Anubis, the jackal-headed god, and Thoth, the ibis-headed god, tended a great balance. The heart of the deceased was placed in one pan. A feather symbolizing *Ma'at*, or truth, was placed in the other pan. If the scale balanced all was well, but if the heart sank in the scales, then the

Egyptian was declared to be heavy with sin. At the foot of the balance a monster, the Devourer, threw himself on the dead one if the judgment went against him. If the judgment was favorable, the Egyptian could start life anew in a paradise called the "Field of Offerings and Reeds," or the "Fields of Yaru." There he could perform the same activities that he had pursued during his lifetime.

In order to enter this eternal life the Egyptian had first to be identified with Osiris and then resurrected in the manner of Osiris. Accordingly, in a series of magical rituals, the dead one became Osiris. He was given the name Osiris in magical funerary papyrus texts placed in the tomb. Moreover, the dead Egyptian had to be embalmed and mummified, as Osiris had been. The body was thus disemboweled, thoroughly dried, and wrapped in linen. Priests supervised the process and recited a series of magical spells at appropriate stages while amulets were placed on the different parts of the mummy's body. Each amulet represented a part of Osiris—for example, the amulet, *tet*, was his backbone. A large scarab beetle symbolizing Khepra, the creator of life, was placed over the heart of the dead one. The entrails of the deceased—liver, lungs, stomach, and intestines—were separately embalmed and placed in four different Canopic jars, each having a lid representing one of the four sons of Horus. These jars were placed in a coffer. The mummy of the deceased was provided with a mask, resembling the live face, and then set within a series of coffins shaped in human form. A rite called "opening the mouth" was performed on the deceased both at his bier and on a black wood statue on the day of the funeral. Outside the tomb, the embalmer, wear- a mask of the jackal-headed god, Anubis, held the mummy upright while a priest touched the face with magical instruments. Previously the same ritual of "opening of the mouth" had been performed in the studio of the sculptor on the statue of the dead one, and also in the embalmer's workshop. The ceremony was designed to animate the dead one and enable his bodily processes to function. Finally, the mummy, as the resurrected Osiris, was laid in the burial chamber—the House of Eternity, as it was called.

The spread and universalization of this cult of Osiris, by which the Egyptian identified his own resurrection and eternality with that of the god, was of the highest historical importance. During most of the Old Kingdom, the privilege of being identified with Osiris, and thus of ensuring resurrection, was restricted to the king, as the lord and ruler of Egypt. However, by the Fifth Dynasty of the Old Kingdom, decentralizing tendencies were already at work which weakened the power of the king and strengthened the hand of the nobles and nomarchs. A visible sign of this decentralization was the change in burial practices of the nobles. Whereas in the Fourth Dynasty the great nobles had desired to be buried near the pyramid of the god-king, by the Sixth Dynasty many of them were erecting separate tombs for themselves in their respective provinces.

First Intermediate Period

With the First Intermediate Period, from the Seventh to the Tenth Dynasties (ca. 2200–2050 B.C.), the Old Kingdom disintegrated. The provincial nobles seized more and more power and unified rule broke down as a great number of small principalities appeared. Adding to the political chaos were raids by Bedouin nomads who crossed the unguarded frontiers and inflicted havoc in the Delta.

In this period of chaos, violence, famine, and disruption, the traditional confidence of the Old Kingdom was severely shaken. For the first time many Egyptians were disillusioned and a distinct note of pessimism crept into some of their writings. Other Egyptians resorted to a deliberate pursuit of pleasure or an attitude of cynicism.

An age of such total disorder brought strong cries and demands for a return to justice, truth, and order—in short, for *Ma'at*. There is some evidence that in the First Intermediary Period this demand for social justice and a return to order and truth was voiced by the lower classes, including the peasants. In any event, the anguish of the common man was heard, and it was loud and insistent. The Egyptian lacked recourse to the living king whose power and prestige had temporarily receded. Yet the power and prestige of the dead king as Osiris remained. Thus Osiris now became not only the dead king but the King of the Dead. His magical power and extraordinary gifts—his charisma—increased greatly. Many nobles saw an opportunity to identify with him in order to achieve that eternality and resurrection heretofore reserved for the god-king. Thus the cult of Osiris came to offer concrete salvation to a new blessed elite—the nobility. And in principle identification with Osiris was now open to anyone, though in practice it was restricted to those who could afford the elaborate funeral rites.

The Middle Kingdom

The First Intermediate Period came to an end when King Mentuhotep I (ca. 2050 B.C.) of the new city of Thebes destroyed the power of rival princes in the city of Heracleopolis, thereby ushering in the Middle Kingdom. Shortly thereafter, another Theban family inaugurated the celebrated Twelfth Dynasty (ca. 1990–1780 B.C.), which was looked upon by later Egyptians as their classical age.

The achievements of the Middle Kingdom were considerable. Egypt was reunified and the archaic foundations of its civilization, centering in divine kingship and *Ma'at* were reasserted. Egypt experienced a new era of stability, prosperity, and creativity under the capable kings of the Twelfth Dynasty, who showed a solicitude for the people that had been lacking among the rulers of the Old Kingdom. This sense of social responsibility was manifested both in the portrait statues of the kings, which reveal in their facial expression a sense of care and concern, and in concrete achievements. The kings undertook vast public works for the benefit of the entire population; one was the gigantic drainage and irrigation project in the Fayum, which reclaimed some twenty-seven thousand acres of arable land. This area became a royal domain containing an enormous building, measuring eight hundred by a thousand feet, which functioned as an administrative and religious center for the whole of Egypt. The building, known as the Labyrinth, was one of the wonders of the ancient world. Unfortunately, both the building and the town which grew up around it have disappeared.

The Egyptian people, like their kings of the Twelfth Dynasty, were imbued with a greater sense of social responsibility and justice. In this period *Ma'at* came to stress the need for heightened concern for and right action toward one's fellow man. In short, it had taken on distinct ethical elements and certain character requirements on the part of the individual. This emphasis was apparent in the manner in which the cult of Osiris flourished in the Middle Kingdom. The possibility of becoming identified with Osiris was now open to every Egyptian. But before the identification could be effected, the deceased had to be judged [4] by a council of gods directed by Re. The judgment was based on a weighing of the good against the evil in the individual's life and the pronouncement of justice. In short, fulfillment of the requirements of ritual was not enough to assure an eternal life after death; the individual must also have lived an ethically correct life.

In the Middle Kingdom the universalization of the cult of Osiris had proceeded to the point where the common man not only identified himself with the god Osiris, but also with the king Osiris. Since the dead king was Osiris, the funerary cult of the people began to imitate the funeral cult of the kings. In the coffins of ordinary people were placed various royal insignia such as crowns and scepters. The democratization of the hereafter allowed the ordinary man to believe that he could participate in the ritual of eternal resurrective recurrence, just as the king could. In a society where eternality was all-important, this was a truly remarkable achievement.

It is apparent that the Middle Kingdom continued the ancient traditions of Egyptian civilization, but gave them new emphases. The kings engaged in important foreign affairs such as the subjugation and annexation of Lower Nubia. They sent expeditions into Palestine and Syria, spreading Egyptian culture in these spheres of influence. The rulers exploited the important mines of Sinai. Dramatic as the foreign adventures and domestic attainments of the Middle Kingdom were, they did not sever Egyptian life from its archaic foundations. The old traditions—based on kingship, the gods, and eternal recurrence—continued in substantially the same forms long after the Middle Kingdom itself had fallen.

[4] In the Middle Kingdom Osiris was not yet the judge of the afterlife, a position he was to attain in the New Kingdom.

THE CHALLENGE OF INTERNATIONAL EMPIRES AND COSMOPOLITAN CULTURE

Midway in the second millennium before Christ, the whole Near East saw a significant and accelerated change. Prior to this time initiative in creating political power and high civilization had rested squarely on the river valley civilizations of Mesopotamia and Egypt. The Egyptians had normally confined themselves to ruling the territory north of the first cataract of the Nile, while the Mesopotamians ruled mainly over peoples in the Tigris-Euphrates valley. On various occasions, however, both Mesopotamia and Egypt had exercised important influence over surrounding barbarian peoples. For example, in the period from about 3000 to 1700 B.C., the Mesopotamians had a decisive impact on the Elamites, who were situated in the territory of the Zagros Mountains, in modern Luristan and Khuzistan, with Susa as their capital. And in the Middle Kingdom of Egypt during the Twelfth Dynasty (ca. 2000–1800 B.C.), lower Nubia was conquered and annexed to Egypt, while the mines in the peninsula of Sinai were systematically exploited. Both Palestine and Syria came into the sphere of Egyptian influence, and relations with princes from Phoenicia and North Syria were carefully cultivated. A preliminary expansion of civilization from the river valley areas was thus already under way prior to 1500 B.C.

After 1500 B.C., the expansion of civilization in the Near East assumed a different character. In the first place, a series of peoples now took the initiative in creating new centers of political power and civilization; and they began to compete with the river valley areas as well as enter into contacts with them. Three principal groups were involved: Indo-Europeans from the North; peoples such as the Hurrians and Kassites who came from the highland areas; and Semites who had migrated from desert regions. Secondly, the various peoples of the ancient Near East were now drawn into much closer contact with each other on many fronts—economic, political, and cultural. These new international contacts were a characteristic phenomenon in the entire Near East after 1500 B.C.

The Indo-Europeans

The invasions of Indo-Europeans, Hurrians and Kassites, and of Semites extended over hundreds of years and must not be thought of as vast incursions of hordes such as the Huns or Mongols. Instead, peoples migrated and infiltrated gradually. The migrations assumed various forms, and even the Indo-European invasions were not all of the same kind.

The Indo-European peoples were so designated because they spoke languages which were ultimately derived from a single parent tongue. Their original home was apparently somewhere in Europe between Scandinavia and the Russian steppes. They were a nomadic people who were probably divided into three social castes—warriors, priests, and peasants. Shortly before 2000 B.C. they left their homeland and began a series of migrations which eventually covered a wide area of Europe, parts of the Near East, and India. In Europe, Indo-Europeans who spoke dialects from which Latin is derived reached Italy, while peoples speaking a related dialect entered Greece.

Several features characterized the Indo-European invasions into the Near East. The actual numbers of the invaders may have been relatively small. More often than not they were nomadic horsemen who functioned as a warrior elite ruling over subject peoples that far outnumbered them. In this task they were aided by such military techniques as the horse-drawn war chariot.

Around 2000 B.C., numbers of Indo-Europeans filtered into Asia Minor. There they came in contact with a native people who spoke Hattic, subdued them, and coalesced into a joint power by around 1700 B.C. They revered the gods of the native (Hattic) peoples in whose areas they had settled, but had their own dominant religion and institutions.

This Indo-European coalition constituted the basis of Hittite culture. After being in Asia Minor for a good 400 or 500 years, the Hittites succeeded in creating a substantial political power—the Hittite Empire—which covered much of Asia Minor and Syria. The Hittites even made a raid on Babylon around 1590 B.C., though they never occupied it or Mesopotamia. The Hittite Empire became a formidable rival to the Egyptian Empire, and did not fall apart until around 1200 B.C., when it succumbed to the sea peoples who invaded it from across the Aegean.

Other Indo-Europeans reached the Iranian plateau either by way of the Caucasus or from central Asia. From Iran, roving bands of Indo-Europeans came into Mesopotamia, where they helped the highland peoples—the Kassites and Hurrians—to organize powerful military attacks against the civilized Mesopotamians. The new groups were for a time held back by the rough terrain around Mesopotamia, and by a strong valley kingdom, but ultimately they succeeded in establishing themselves among the valley peoples.

The Kassites, who came from the Zagros mountain lands near the border of Persia, organized a state which threatened the successors of Hammurabi in central Mesopotamia. Aided by Indo-Europeans, they succeeded in establishing themselves in the Mesopotamian plain, under King Agum (ca. 1645–1624 B.C.). The Kassites had taken advantage of the Hittite raid on Babylon around 1590 B.C. After the Hittite withdrawal, the Kassites took possession of Babylon and established a Third Babylonian Dynasty which lasted for at least 500 years (ca. 1600–1100 B.C.)

The Hurrians, known in the Bible as Horites, may have originally stemmed from the highlands of Armenia. Flourishing in the Near East between approximately 2500 and 1000 B.C., they participated in the maintenance of a Mitanni Empire which reached its height around 1500 B.C. An Indo-Iranian elite of chariot warriors must have played a decisive role in the creation of the Mitanni Empire, since we know that the leaders were Indo-Iranian nobility (*maryannu*). The center of this empire was the Middle Euphrates Valley near Harran; from this strategically advantageous position, the Hurrians dominated the region of Assyria. In addition, they overran parts of Asia Minor, Syria, and Palestine, but in these regions they did not organize enduring kingdoms. The Hurrians adopted much of Mesopotamian culture and served as intermediaries in spreading it to such peoples as the Hittites.

The effects of the Indo-European invasions were also felt in Egypt. By the seventeenth century B.C. the pressure of the Hittites had been felt in Syria and had created dislocations of Semitic peoples in Syria and Canaan. Caught between the Mediterranean Sea and the desert, bands of Semites, who were in contact with both Indo-Europeans and Hurrians, infiltrated the Egyptian Delta. These invaders were known as the Hyksos. On present evidence the Hyksos were predominantly Semitic, although Indo-European and Hurrian elements were also present. They actually controlled only the Delta but could dominate an Egypt that had become progressively weakened during the latter phase of the Middle Kingdom. The period of Hyksos domination in Egypt extended from 1720 to 1570 B.C.

The Hyksos introduced new techniques of warfare into Egypt during their period of domination. These included the horse-drawn chariot, a more powerful and heavier type of sword, body armor, and a special rectangular fortress made out of beaten earth. Some of these techniques show the Indo-European influence. Although the Hyksos attempted to adapt to Egyptian civilization, the Egyptians in official propaganda pictured them as the hated enemy par excellence.

The New International Empires

A most important manifestation of the closer political contacts between peoples in the Near East after the middle of the second millennium was the creation of a number of international empires. The imperial urge was not, of course, a new thing; it had already been manifested in Sargon of Akkad, Naram-Sin, and the Egyptian Middle Kingdom. But the new international empires flourished within a larger, more complex, and more cosmopolitan context. A series of these empires including the Egyptian, Hittite, Assyrian, Chaldean or Neo-Babylonian, and Persian dominated the Near East from 1570 B.C. until the conquests of Alexander the Great (333–329 B.C.). The international empire became in this period the *normal* political form in the Near East and was characterized by the fact that it was "ruled by one nation which made other peoples subject and tributary." Between the crystallizations of these empires, there were interludes in which small nations such as the Hebrew and Phoenician enjoyed temporary independence, and sometimes even aspired to the creation of empires of their own—as did the Hebrews under Solomon. But usually their independence lasted only a short while. They were quickly absorbed into one of the great imperial systems as the conquering nations sought to achieve stability in size. The best example of political imperialism in this age of oriental empires was the Persian Empire (539–331 B.C.), which finally succeeded in uniting all the peoples of the ancient Near East under its hegemony.

The creation of these international empires was

made possible in part by important technical advances in military weaponry and tactics, the natural instability of the earlier kingdoms in the river valleys, increasing population, accumulated experience in long-range administration, and the impact of migrations by peoples such as the Indo-Europeans. Clearly the Near East was in ferment, and its peoples were driven to experiment not only in politics, technology, and society, but in culture and religion as well. A new cultural universalism found expression in the invention of the alphabet and in the spread of such languages as Aramean and Akkadian as international vehicles of communication. The rulers of the great empires built huge capital cities as symbols of their power and wealth. In religion the Hebrews broke basically with the mythical nature gods of the Egyptians and Mesopotamians by postulating a God of universal history. In Persia a new cosmopolitan religion emerged with Zoroaster, the prophet.

The civilizations of Mesopotamia and Egypt also participated in the experiments in imperialism and cosmopolitanism that characterized the period after 1500 B.C. In the religious sphere they remained characteristically conservative. Both Mesopotamia and Egypt maintained vital links with their archaic pasts during this interval. The Mesopotamians responded to the new challenges as they had had to respond to earlier invading peoples, such as the Akkadians. These had been absorbed and had assimilated the basic cultural pattern of Mesopotamian civilization. The same process of assimilation occurred after the incursions of Indo-Europeans, Kassites, and Hurrians. The subsequent development of the Assyrian, Neo-Chaldean, and Persian empires did not *fundamentally* disrupt the continuity of Mesopotamian cultural values, though significant changes did take place in political outlook and organization. Nor did the Hyksos invasions or the formation of the Egyptian Empire during the New Kingdom fundamentally alter the cultural constants of archaic Egyptian civilization.

It is necessary now to examine a few of the major political and cultural developments in the ancient Near East from the time of the Egyptian Empire, 1570 B.C., to the conquests of Alexander the Great from 333 to 329 B.C.

The first phase of international empires lasted from about 1500 to 1200 B.C. During this period a struggle for control of the Palestine-Syria corridor took place between the greatest empire of the period—the Egyptians—and their rivals, the Hittites. Farther east, in Assyria, a separate power struggle ensued between the Mitanni Empire and a rising new power, the first Assyrian Empire. These four empires illustrate the two different ways that international empires were created. The Hittite and Mitanni Empires were created by intruders who seized the initiative and imposed their rule on native civilized peoples. The Egyptian and first Assyrian Empires, on the other hand, were the result of native reactions to invasions by outsiders. The Egyptian Empire was a response to the thrust of the Hyksos invaders, and the native Assyrians reacted to the conquest of their land by the Hurrians.

In Egypt, the strong reaction to the invasion of the Hyksos was decisively aided by new techniques and weapons of warfare that the Egyptians had acquired from their conquerors. The Egyptian King of Thebes, Kamose, pushed the Hyksos back into the Delta (ca. 1580 B.C.); and his successor, Ahmose I, finally expelled them and founded the Eighteenth Dynasty and the New Kingdom. With the triumph of an imperialistic, warlike party in Egypt under

Thut-mose III (ca. 1490–1436 B.C.), an Egyptian Empire was consolidated. In seventeen successive years Thut-mose led seventeen campaigns into Syria, his empire even reaching the Euphrates. Under his successors, Egypt was the greatest state of the Near East. In the time of Amenhotep III (ca. 1398–1361 B.C.), the Mitanni Empire, which bordered the Egyptian Empire on the Euphrates, was an ally of the Egyptians; and Babylonian, Assyrian, and Hittite kings sent gifts and letters to the Pharaoh acknowledging his power. The territory outside of Egypt in Palestine and Syria was garrisoned by Egyptian troops, governed by Egyptian high commissioners, and served by an Egyptian courier system. The basic policy of the pharaohs, beginning with Thut-mose III, was to allow local princes to remain on their thrones, but to take their sons to Egypt as hostages. The sons, in turn, were brought up at the Egyptian court and then sent home to rule as vassal kings.

Under Pharaoh Amenhotep IV (ca. 1369–1353 B.C.), the energies of the Egyptians were mainly absorbed in an internal struggle for power between the king and the priests of Amen. The Empire being temporarily weakened, disaffection arose in Syria and Palestine. The Hittites' powerful ruler, Suppiluliumash (ca. 1380–1347 B.C.), conquered inner Asia Minor and perhaps advanced to the Aegean; to the east he extended himself to Armenia and Assyria. The Hittites now moved south into Syria, and the Palestinian region disintegrated into a number of small independent states.

Under Rameses II (ca. 1290–1224 B.C.), the Egyptians made an attempt to reconquer Palestine and Syria, engaging in a long war against the Hittites. Finally, around 1270 B.C. the two sides concluded a peace treaty whereby the Hittites held Syria, while the Egyptians regained Palestine. The new peace was cemented in 1257 B.C. when Rameses II married the Hittite king's daughter. Nevertheless, both Egypt and the Hittites had seriously weakened themselves by the war. Sea peoples from the Aegean attacked the Hittites and destroyed them. Egypt, too, was threatened but managed to maintain her independence, though she declined seriously for about 400 years.

The entire age of oriental empires was characterized by the struggle of new universalistic and cosmopolitan values and institutions against archaic traditions. This struggle can be graphically illustrated by the history of Egypt during this imperial period. The creation of an Egyptian Empire in Asiatic Syria and Palestine brought with it numerous changes. Many Egyptians now began to live in Palestine and Syria; conversely, Asiatics came into Egypt in much larger numbers as hostages and laborers. Cultural and trade contacts between Egyptians and Asiatics quickened. Foreign words crept into the Egyptian language. Art became more naturalistic and lost some of its archaic stylization. In architecture the power and ostentation of the age were manifested by the creation of temples that were gigantic in size, wealth, and influence, like the temple complex of Karnak. In the Amarna Period of the Egyptian Empire (ca. 1375–1353 B.C.), new tendencies revealed themselves in the Egyptian state respecting the pharaoh, the army, the civil service bureaucracy, and the priesthood.

The pharaoh was still regarded as a god, but he had lost some of his vast authority. Wilson has shown that, increasingly, three competing groups encroached upon his power. One was the professional army with a separate commander stationed abroad and hence not subject to direct supervision and control. Such an army had the potential of becoming an independent force. Secondly, the Egyptian civil service, with its own special interests and techniques of rule, now developed on a vast scale. It, too, was potentially dangerous to the pharaoh, if its interests and those of the ruler should clash. Thirdly, the priesthoods gained enormously in power and wealth. The priesthoods of Re at Heliopolis, of Ptah at Memphis, and Amen-Re at Thebes, were powerful and affluent organizations. In particular, the cause of the god Amen flourished with the rise of the New Kingdom. Amen came to be looked upon as a national god of victory and the god of the empire. He was syncretically identified with the sun god and designated as Amen-Re. At Karnak, the temple complex symbolized the power and success attained by Amen-Re and his priesthood.

In the reign of the Pharaoh Amenhotep IV (ca. 1369–1353 B.C.), a revolution occurred which took the specific form of a struggle between the king and the priests of Amen. In the sixth year of his reign, Amenhotep IV undertook to introduce into Egypt a form of religion based on monotheism—the worship of Aton, or disk of the sun, as the sole god. This brought him into conflict with the priesthood of Thebes, who supported Amen-Re. He changed his name from Amenhotep (Amen is satisfied) to Akhenaton (It is well with Aton), and gave up Thebes as the capital city to establish a new one, Akhetaton, near Tell el-Amarna, about 200 miles north of Thebes. There he set up his court and devoted himself to the "new" religion, ordering his agents to go through the length and breadth of Egypt and efface the names of all other gods, particularly Amen.

The whole problem of the religion of Akhenaton is

complex and controversial. There are differing views both
as to the reasons for the movement and its nature. There
are those who regard Akhenaton as a creative genius who
forged a new religion. Others see nothing particularly
novel in the movement and even contend that Akhenaton
did not break with traditional Egyptian religious practices.
Certainly, conflict with the priests of Amen was an important factor in producing Akhenaton's "new" tendencies.
But this conflict had begun earlier, in the time of Akhenaton's father, and was even reflected in the reign of Thut-
mose IV (ca. 1406–1398 B.C.). The monotheism of Akhenaton thus seems to have been an attempt to reduce the
power of the Amen cult by reviving other, depressed cults,
especially the sun cults of Heliopolis.

Those who emphasize the originality of this new
religion should take note, as John A. Wilson has observed,
that many of its elements were not new at all. Sun worship
was very old in Egypt, and the specific worship of Aton
had begun at least two generations before Akhenaton.
Even hymns addressed to a single god were present in
Egyptian religion long before this time. And as for the
universalism of the god Aton, another eminent authority,
William C. Hayes, has emphasized that this had already
been present in solar worship under Amenhotep III (ca.
1398–1361 B.C.).

Four additional things should be noted about Atonism. First, the god Aton, the disk of the sun, was a nature
god and like the traditional mythic Egyptian gods, never
transcended nature but was essentially an embodiment of
it. Second, Aton was not primarily an ethical god. Third,
while Akhenaton worshipped only one god in what seems
to have been an uncompromising monotheism, this was
not true of his followers at Amarna. While they regarded
Aton as a god, they also worshipped the pharaoh as a god-

king. Thus not even the immediate followers of Akhenaton could break with the fundamental Egyptian notion of the divinity of the pharaoh. Fourth, the whole experiment with Atonism was an interesting but temporary episode; in the end it failed completely. Under a successor, Tutankhaton (ca. 1352–1344 B.C.), the old forces in Egypt won out. In fact, Tutankhaton changed his name to Tutankhamen, abandoned the city of Akhetaton and returned to Thebes, and there made complete submission to the old gods. Egypt thus returned to her traditional ways in religion. In art the short-lived naturalistic experiments in sculpture and painting of Akhenaton's reign were replaced by the traditional archaic stylization.

During the late New Kingdom and in succeeding periods Egyptian religion became increasingly ritualistic and magical. This tendency is reflected in the funerary texts that were placed in the dead person's tomb—The Books of the Dead—intended to guide the individual in the afterlife. Composed by the priests, they contained magical formulae for identifying the dead person with Osiris, for frustrating the magical powers of his enemies, for transforming the dead one into other forms and powers, and so on. The cult of Osiris thus increasingly lost its ethical import and, like most other aspects of Egyptian religion, took on a magical-ritualistic character.

The Age of Small Nations: Philistines, Phoenicians, Arameans, and Hebrews

The next phase in the age of the empires, beginning during the twelfth century, was a fateful one. Since the Hittite Empire had been destroyed, Assyria reduced to a weak power, and Egypt had retreated back into its shell, there was no great power in the Near East during the twelfth century. This not only gave mobility to various peoples, but enabled a number of them to establish small sovereignties in the lands vacated by once great powers. Four may be singled out—the Philistines, the Phoenicians, the Hebrews, and the Arameans—all of whom established themselves in the Syrian-Palestine corridor.

The Philistines, unlike the Phoenicians, Arameans, and Hebrews, were not originally Semitic desert nomads. Instead, they were part of the invasion by sea peoples from across the Aegean Sea. They may have come from the island of Crete; at least biblical tradition accepts them as coming from Caphtor, which is the Hebrew name for Crete. In any event, they established themselves on the coastal plain of Palestine between Jappa and the Wadi Ghazzeh. Prior to the time of David, the second King of Israel (ca. 1000–962 B.C.), the Philistines lived in some five independent cities, ruled by "lords." After their defeat by David, they were ruled by kings. The Philistines left no significant culture and functioned mainly as a thorn in the side of the Hebrews with whom they frequently warred.

The Phoenicians established themselves along the Mediterranean coast in such cities as Byblos, Sidon, Berytos, and Tyre. Phoenicia was about 120 miles long and very narrow, with the Lebanon Mountains forming a natural barrier to the east. The southern border was Mt. Carmel where Phoenicia adjoined Israel. While their land was fertile, it was too narrow to support the population. Hence the Phoenicians turned to the sea and became the great international sea traders of the ancient Near East. They were masters of the sea routes of the eastern Mediterranean, and even extended themselves into the western Mediterranean as far as Spain. They established colonies in such areas as Sicily and North Africa, with Carthage becoming the most famous.

The Phoenician cities were important trading and industrial centers. Their chief product, from which they derived enormous wealth, was a purple dye produced from the sea snail murex found in the Mediterranean. In addition, they exported glass, weapons, wine, and the famous woods from Lebanon. The important Ras Shamra Texts from the ancient Mediterranean city of Ugarit have established that Phoenician religion was a form of the Canaanite religion of the West Semites. They worshipped a pantheon of gods, including El and his consort Asherah, a mother goddess, and the youthful fertility god Baal also played a decisive role.

The Phoenicians exemplified the universalism and internationalism of the age of empires; in international trade they served as intermediaries between the peoples of the Near East and the western Mediterranean, incidentally spreading the alphabet and the Babylonian system of weights and measures.

A third people, desert Semites who settled in Syria, Palestine, and northern Mesopotamia, were the Arameans. On land they played a role similar to that of the Phoenicians on the sea, becoming the great international caravan traders of the Near East. From Damascus, a key head and terminus of many trade routes, the Arameans extended their activities as merchants and cultural middlemen to Iraq, Arabia, and Egypt. They absorbed cultural ingredients, adapted them, and spread them with amazing facility. From the Phoenicians, for example, they derived the alphabet, adapted it to their own needs, and in a spectacular process of transmission, spread it to the Persians, the Hebrews, and other peoples. The cuneiform scripts of the Akkadians and Persians, which had attained an international status and were widely used, eventually gave way before the superiority of Aramean alphabetical writing.

Thus, even after the Arameans were conquered by the new Assyrian Empire in the eighth century B.C., Aramean trade continued to be a leading factor in the Near East, and their language became the common tongue in that area. Jesus spoke it in his home.

A fourth people who settled in the Palestine-Syrian area, the Hebrews, were destined to play a world-shaking role in history out of all proportion to their numbers and political significance. This was due of course to their religion. An account of the Hebrews is outside the scope of this book.[1] But the reader should observe that the God of the Hebrews was a god who manifested his will not only in nature but also in history. He was a god who put upon both individual men and whole peoples ethical and historical obligations of a kind never even conceived in the magical mythopoeic outlook of Mesopotamia and Egypt.

In the twelfth century before the birth of Christ, while Philistines, Phoenicians, Arameans, and Hebrews were organizing in the Palestine-Syrian corridor, other tribal peoples, such as the Medes and Chaldeans, were gradually infiltrating into Iran and southern Mesopotamia respectively. The Medes spoke an Indo-Iranian form of Indo-European language, while the Chaldeans spoke a Semitic language related to that of the Arameans.

The New Empires: Assyrians, Chaldeans, and Persians

By about 1100 B.C. a new power constellation was slowly taking shape, the second Assyrian Empire. Under a series of able rulers, including Ashur-nasir-pal II (883–

[1] Another volume in this series, *The Judaeo-Christian Tradition*, by J. H. Hexter, is recommended for the reader who wishes to study the Hebrews in some detail.

859 B.C.), Tiglath-Pileser III (745–727 B.C.), Sargon II
(722–705 B.C.), Sennacherib (705–681 B.C.), Esarhaddon
(681–668 B.C.), and Ashur-bani-pal (668–625 B.C.), the
Assyrians fashioned a truly formidable international power.
At its greatest extension under Ashur-bani-pal, the Assyrians controlled all of Mesopotamia and Elam, a part
of the Iranian plateau, portions of Asia Minor, Syria, and
Palestine, and Egypt as far as Thebes. But this second
Assyrian Empire led a precarious existence, and a short
time after Ashur-bani-pal it collapsed. In 612 B.C. a coalition of enemies, made up of Chaldeans led by King Nabo-
polassar of Babylon, Medes from Iran under Cyaxares, and
barbarian nomads from the north—the Scythians—captured and destroyed the Assyrian capital of Nineveh. By
605 B.C. Assyria had ceased to exist as a nation, and the
Assyrian people quickly disappeared from the pages of
history.

The strength of the Assyrian Empire rested on a
number of factors. A sturdy peasant people, the Assyrians
were vigorous fighters, and a number of their kings were
able military leaders. Besides, the Assyrians created the
first large-scale armies totally equipped with weapons of
iron. Archers and heavy-armed spearmen and shield-
bearers, together with cavalry and war chariots, battering
rams, and siege equipment, constituted a powerful war
machine. In addition, the Assyrians "systematically" utilized
terror as a permanent instrument of warfare.

Basically, the empire was held together by military
power. The subject peoples were always waiting for an
opportunity to revolt. Sometimes the Assyrians adopted the
Egyptian technique of using vassal kings, but they also
divided their empire into provinces ruled by Assyrian
governors. They practiced deportation, often shifting whole
peoples from one part of the empire to another when-

ever they caused too much trouble. Yet it would be a mistake to view the Assyrians as solely preoccupied with terror and the maintenance of military supremacy. Assyrian culture belied this. It was a hybrid, assimilating much from the earlier Mesopotamian culture of the Sumerians, Akkadians, Amorites, and Babylonians. In addition, the Assyrians adapted elements from other peoples such as the Phoenicians, adding some genuine contributions of their own.

While the Assyrians were not merely slavish imitators and sometimes modified the earlier traditions, the leading characteristic of their culture was its fundamental continuity with previous Mesopotamian traditions and values. Indeed, the Assyrians, as well as the Babylonian Chaldeans who succeeded them, self-consciously regarded themselves as the custodians of the archaic culture of the Sumerians and Babylonians.[2] This was the role they cast for themselves, and it was a role that they were proud of. Thus the great Assyrian King Ashur-bani-pal gathered together an enormous library, a portion of which was made up of the literary masterpieces of the Mesopotamian past. On thousands of clay tablets, written in cuneiform, a significant legacy of the Mesopotamian past was preserved and venerated. Our knowledge of many of the Mesopotamian myths and epics comes from such tablet finds. The respect for the archaic tradition of Mesopotamia was likewise revealed by Ashur-bani-pal when, upon capturing

[2] The many political antagonisms between Assyrians and Babylonians should not blind one to the basic cultural continuity between the two peoples. And, as Ephraim Speiser has argued, other differences between Babylonia and Assyria in matters of physical environment, aspects of law, customs and dress, economy, and art and architecture, still could not eliminate their common cultural tradition.

the Elamite city of Susa, he recorded that he was able to recover the statue of the goddess Nana which an Elamite king had taken from Uruk 1635 years earlier.

The archaic mold was also manifest again and again in Assyrian religion. For example, the Assyrian attitude toward their temples was thoroughly archaic. Since the temple represented a covenant between a god and his community, it was necessary that the temple's original foundations never be destroyed or radically modified. In this, as in most things, restoration rather than change characterized the Assyrian attitude. Thus a temple that had been damaged by warfare had to be restored on its original foundations and never built in a new place.

The cultural continuum was likewise exhibited in the pantheons of the gods among the Assyrians and Chaldeans. These gods were really the old Sumerian gods of heaven, air, and earth, and retained the same names— Anu, Enlil, and Ea, or Enki. Similarly, the three astral gods of the Assyrians and Chaldeans were the sun, the moon, and Venus, although here their names were changed from the Sumerian. They were called Shamash, Sin, and Ishtar. The national god of the Assyrians, Ashur, was distinctly Assyrian, representing both the name of the people and the capital; but, in general, there was a remarkable continuity between the Sumerian religious tradition and the Assyrian pantheon.

An outstanding achievement of the Assyrians was their art, which in part continued previous Mesopotamian forms and traditions. Although they had plentiful supplies of stone, they followed the earlier Mesopotamian use of brick for most of their buildings, including temples. After 2000 B.C. the Assyrians gradually evolved a fairly distinct style, the most noteworthy feature being relief sculpture.

Here the religious element played a subordinate role. True, the Assyrians employed great winged figures that presided at ritual scenes. On the other hand, reliefs designed to decorate the palace of the Assyrian rulers made initial use of secular and narrative motifs, and emphasized two themes—war and hunting. These reliefs were done with realism, power, and the capacity to portray such emotions as cruelty, rage, and agony, with remarkable unity of effect and intensity. The hunting scenes of King Ashur-bani-pal are true masterpieces! Such Assyrian art illustrated the tendency of all Mesopotamian art to emphasize natural scenery. And yet Assyrian art, for all of its realism, did not free itself of certain archaic Mesopotamian conventions. It lacked, for example, a sense of perspective and always represented figures in profile.

The fall of the Assyrian Empire in 612 B.C. provided an opportunity for a new group of smaller empires and kingdoms to come to the fore. The Assyrian Empire was basically divided between the Medes and the Chaldeans. The Medes, originally a tribal people, now created a modest empire made up of the Median Kingdom in the Iranian plateau, plus the former possessions of Assyria in Asia Minor. The Chaldeans, also originally a tribal people, established the Chaldean, or Neo-Babylonian Empire (612–539 B.C.), and ruled over Mesopotamia, Syria, and Palestine. The Egyptians, led by the Pharaoh Necho II, attempted to stop the Chaldeans at Carchemish in Syria, but were defeated by the Chaldean king, Nebuchadrezzar (605 B.C.). This Chaldean king also punished the kingdom of Judah in Palestine for joining Egypt against him; he eventually destroyed Jerusalem in 586 B.C. after previous attempts to pacify Judah. Meanwhile, in western Asia Minor, a prosperous state—the kingdom of Lydia—thrived during this time.

The independence of these smaller kingdoms and empires of the Near East was destroyed by a new colossus —the Persian Empire. Ironically enough, this largest and most cosmopolitan state of the ancient Near East was not established by a native Near Eastern people, but by Indo-Europeans—the Persians—who were related to the Medes. Led by King Cyrus the Persians rebelled against their former suzerains, the Medes, defeating and gaining control over them in 549 B.C. Cyrus then embarked upon a brilliant series of conquests (550–529 B.C.). He faced a combination of enemies including Lydia, Chaldea, and Sparta. Utilizing Assyrian military techniques, he struck a death blow at Lydia in Asia Minor and subdued the Lydians, captured their capital, Sardis, and reached the southern shores of Asia Minor by 546 B.C. He next attacked the Chaldean or Neo-Babylonian Empire and easily defeated the Chaldean ruler, Nabonidus, taking Babylon in 538 B.C.

After the death of Cyrus, who fell in battle against barbarian nomads, his son, Cambyses, conquered Egypt, the last remaining power in the Near East, in 525 B.C. Thus, in an amazing period of twenty-five years, Cyrus and his son had carved out an empire that embraced all the peoples of the ancient Near East. Under Darius (521–486 B.C.), Persian rule extended from the shores of the Nile in Egypt to beyond the Indus River in India.

The Persian emperor was faced with the task of governing many subject peoples. Darius, successor to Cambyses, undertook to reorganize the Persian provincial system, which lasted until the time of Alexander the Great (334 B.C.). He divided the empire into twenty administrative units known as satrapies. These provinces were governed by satraps—governors appointed by the emperor; they came from noble families or sometimes the royal family itself and they enjoyed extensive civil, judicial, and financial powers, as well as a certain autonomy in foreign policy and local matters. The armed forces of each satrapy were under the control of a local military commander. The central government checked on the local governments by means of officials known as the king's eye or the king's ear, who also kept an eye out for signs of rebellion. The Persian Empire was generally tolerant toward local peoples, so long as they did not attempt rebellion, paid their regularized tribute, and furnished recruits for the royal army.

The Persian provincial system was an improvement over that of the Assyrian Empire. For the first time a vast empire had been created which ruled over a motley group of races and peoples and attempted to give its subjects a measure of equal rights and responsibilities. Naturally, the Persians ruled as an elite and enjoyed preferential treatment in exemptions from taxation and the privileges of holding office. In addition, the Persians used a variety of techniques to weld their empire together. These included a vast system of royal roads, a royal courier and mail service to improve communication, the use of Aramaic as the universal language of Persian administration in the Western half of the empire (and probably in parts of the Eastern half as well), the use of coinage and gold currency which circulated freely throughout the empire, the introduction of the practical Egyptian calendar as a standard for the Persian government, and a royal capital together with various royal residences.

The capital and chief royal residence of the Persian kings was Susa, the ancient Elamite city, though during the colder months Babylon was a favorite residence. Darius also established a residence at Persepolis; the royal tombs of Darius, Xerxes, and other Persian rulers were eventually located nearby.

Persian culture was highly syncretic and eclectic. In architecture, for example, the Persians fused diverse Near Eastern styles and practices. Persian palaces were built on terraces in the Babylonian fashion; the winged bulls at the palace gates were taken from the Assyrians; the vast colonnades of their halls derived from Egypt. This eclecticism in architecture was consonant with the more general cultural eclecticism of the age of empires.

The most original cultural contribution of the Persians was their religion—Zoroastrianism—founded by the prophet Zoroaster, whose exact dates are unknown, although he flourished sometime between 628 and 551 B.C. Zoroastrianism became the official religion of the Persian Empire after the middle of the sixth century B.C. The religion was both monotheistic and dualistic. The prophet Zoroaster proclaimed that there was one supreme god in the universe, a god who created all things material and spiritual, and, in this sense, he was a believer in monotheism. But he also taught that the world was divided between what he called the Truth and the Lie. The Truth was the creation of Ahura Mazda, the Wise Lord, the one god. The origin of the Lie was not indicated by Zoroaster.[3] Truth and Lie, Goodness and Evil, were opposing principles in the world and represented a dualism of opposites. God's creatures were free to choose between the two. The spirit of the Good, of Truth, was called *Spenta Mainyu*, or the Holy Spirit, while that of Evil or the Lie was *Angra Mainyu*, the destructive spirit. These two spirits also possessed free will as did men. Zoroaster boldly proclaimed man's freedom to make ethical choices and therefore his responsibility for his final situation. If he chose

[3] In later Zoroastrian tradition, the origin of the Lie was attributed to Ahriman.

Goodness and the Truth, he would earn an eternal reward in heaven in the form of Wholeness and Immortality. Those who chose Evil or the Lie would suffer the eternal torment of Hell.

Thus did the prophet Zoroaster proclaim his message; it was peculiarly suitable for the universal Persian Empire. This religion apparently did not borrow mythopoeic notions from either Mesopotamia or Egypt, but was Indo-European in origin. In the course of time, however, it underwent significant changes. A most important development was the spread of the Iranian cult of Mithra, the aide and helper of the one god, Ahura Mazda, to various regions of western Asia and Asia Minor. Eventually Mithra, the hero of light, changed into Mithra, the sacrificial sun god, who became the central figure in an important mystery religion that competed with Christianity for the souls of men in the Roman Empire.

Zoroastrianism probably had a large influence on postexilic Judaism. Many experts contend that the emphasis in postexilic Judaism on rewards and punishment, heaven and hell, the struggle between the forces of good and evil, and the notion of an individual afterlife were derived from Zoroastrianism. There is a striking similarity between the *Manual of Discipline* of the Dead Sea community and Zoroastrianism regarding the problem of evil. But other scholars maintain that there is enough in Pharasaic Judaism to justify the search for the origins of these ideas within Palestinian traditions specifically, or even exclusively.

The Persian Empire as the universal state of the ancient Near East ultimately had to confront the Greek city-states in the Persian Wars (546–466 B.C.) and bear the onslaught of the Macedonian Alexander the Great in the

Hellenistic Age. But even then its culture did not disappear. Hellenistic civilization was itself a product of the fusion of Greek and Near Eastern cultural traditions. Rome ultimately subdued the entire eastern Mediterranean and incorporated it into an empire even greater than that of the Persians. In the end, when the Romans had to choose between saving their own lands and traditions and maintaining the Eastern Empire, they chose the latter. Rome's successors, Byzantine and Arab, felt the force of Persian ideas and institutions, and insofar as these new cultures influenced Europe in the Middle Ages, not even the West escaped the impact of ancient Near Eastern civilization.

SELECTED BIBLIOGRAPHY OF

PAPERBOUND EDITIONS

NOTE: This bibliography does not include books on the Old Testament and ancient Judaism, except for a few which deal in some detail with the archaic civilizations of the ancient Near East. For a more extensive bibliographical list of books dealing with the Bible and Judaism, see another work in this series, J. H. Hexter, *The Judaeo-Christian Tradition* (Harper & Row, 1966).

ARCHAEOLOGY, MYTH, AND SOCIAL ANALYSIS

Since the end of World War II, ancient Near Eastern studies have profited from a revolution in archaeological studies, new developments in the study of myth, and important advances in theory of social analysis. The student who wishes to inform himself on the results of these advances should bear in mind the following questions: What are the techniques of archaelogical investigation? What kinds of imaginative exercises are necessary to make the materials yield up their information? What differences are there between the approach of the historian and that of the archaeologist? What is the difference between the "old" and the "new" archaeology? What assumptions, if any, must we make about the intellectual workings of the mind of ancient man if we are to profit from the mass of facts that have been revealed by archaeological digs? What is the nature of myth? Why is myth so important in the ancient Near East? What insights does myth give us into the way ancient peoples looked at themselves and the world around them? How is it possible for people to think mythopoeically on one level, empirically on another, and mathematically on a third level? Are there general social categories or techniques for analyzing any society past or present? In what respects does ancient society resemble modern society? Are social forms dependent upon material factors, especially economic, for their basic configurations, or does the reverse relationship hold, i.e., does the material factor depend upon the psychological and spiritual intentions, purposes, or aims of a civilization? These and a host of related questions are dealt with in the following works.

ARCHAEOLOGY

CHILDE, V. GORDON. *A Short Introduction to Archaeology* (Collier, 1962). Childe, one of the world's leading archaeologists, provides the essential outlines for undertaking an archaeological investigation and shows how to classify and interpret the results. Emphasis is placed on the importance of material factors and artifacts. A brilliant but one-sided approach.

CLARK, GRAHAME. *Archaeology and Society* (University Paperbacks, 1961). An extremely thoughtful and provocative account of archaeology as the systematic study of man's antiquities, showing how a reliable account can be reconstructed, and how this reconstruction constitutes the prelude to the later emergence of history and society.

GRAY, JOHN. *Archaeology and the Old Testament World* (Harper & Row, 1965). A fine account of the archaeology of the entire ancient Near East by a highly competent biblical scholar and archaeologist.

HEIZER, ROBERT (ed). *Man's Discovery of His Past* (Spectrum, 1962). A good collection of writings on the history of archaeology. Provides the student with an excellent perspective on how man has rediscovered his past through archaeology, especially in changing notions of time and change, and the discovery of ancient implements.

KENYON, KATHLEEN M. *Beginning in Archaeology* (Praeger, 1961). Provides fundamental accurate information on archaeological methods and procedures. Gives the student a description of the actual techniques used in diggings, and advice on preparing for a career in archaeology; by a veteran archaeologist.

PIGGOTT, STUART. *Approach to Archaeology* (McGraw-Hill, 1965). One of the best introductions to the entire field of archaeology. Reliable and authoritative, it describes the distinctive method, contribution, and techniques of the archaeologist.

MYTH

CASSIRER, ERNST. *Language and Myth* (Dover, 1946). A brief version of Cassirer's ideas on myth as a symbolic form.

CASSIRER, ERNST. *Philosophy of Symbolic Forms*, Volume 2: *Mythical Thought* (Yale, 1965). A brilliant and profound analysis of myth and mythical thinking by a leading modern philosopher whose range and knowledge were truly universal. His book is of first importance, though it will be difficult reading for the beginning student.

ELIADE, MIRCEA. *Cosmos and History: The Myth of Eternal Return* (Harper & Row, 1959). Eliade centers his discussion of myth on the notion of eternal recurrence and shows the central role it played in archaic societies. This is not an easy book, but the student will be amply rewarded if he masters its arguments and suggestive insights.

ELIADE, MIRCEA. *The Sacred and the Profane* (Harper & Row, 1961). A valuable discussion of religious myth, symbolism, and ritual in culture. The author draws from a wealth of data on religious and social history, psychology, anthropology, and sociology. He is especially good on the nature of sacred time and myths, and the sacredness of nature and cosmic religion.

FRANKFORT, HENRI, ET AL. *Before Philosophy* (Penguin, 1949). A series of essays written by leading authorities on the role of myth in the ancient Near East. The sections by Henri Frankfort and his wife on the nature of myth, John A. Wilson on Egypt, and Thorkild Jacobsen on Mesopotamia are brilliant. Despite the numerous and important criticisms of this work by the noted Sumerologist, Samuel Kramer [in *Journal of Cuneiform Studies*, II (1948), 39–70], this book remains the most significant contribution to the understanding of myth in the ancient Near East.

FRAZER, JAMES. *The New Golden Bough*, edited and abridged by Theodor Gaster (Anchor, 1964). Sir James Frazer

(1854–1941) was one of the world's leading anthropologists. *The Golden Bough* in its expanded form (1915) reached to thirteen volumes and still constitutes the classic repository of materials on cults, myths, and rites. This is a one-volume abridged version brought up to date by the eminent scholar, Theodor Gaster; a fascinating and inexhaustible work.

GASTER, THEODOR. *Thespis: Ritual, Myth and Drama in the Ancient Near East* (Anchor, 1961). A pioneering book which draws upon Egyptian, Hittite, and Canaanite texts to explain the relationship between seasonal rituals, myth, and drama. Difficult reading, but illustrative of new directions in the exploration of myth.

HOOKE, SAMUEL. *Middle-Eastern Mythology* (Penguin, 1963). A good discussion of the different types of myth such as the ritual myth and the myth of origin. Includes also summaries and analyses of Mesopotamian, Egyptian, Ugaritic, and Hittite mythology.

KRAMER, SAMUEL (ed.). *Mythologies of the Ancient World* (Anchor, 1961). An important symposium by ten leading scholars using up-to-date translations. Includes sections on Egypt, Sumer and Akkad, the Hittites, Canaanites, and ancient Iran; attempts to incorporate some of Kramer's criticisms of Frankfort.

MALINOWSKI, BRONISLAW. *Magic, Science and Religion and Other Essays* (Doubleday, 1954). The section in this book on "Myth in Primitive Psychology" is important. Malinowski exercised a significant influence on modern anthropology and was a leader of the "functional" as opposed to the older "evolutionary" approach to the field.

SEBEOK, THOMAS A. (ed.). *Myth: A Symposium* (Midland, 1965). Claude Lévi-Strauss, Dorothy Eggan, Stanley Hyman, and Stith Thompson are among the anthropologists, literary critics, folklorists, and philosophers who bring fresh and stimulating viewpoints to bear on the origin and function of myths in ancient and contemporary civilization.

SOCIAL ANALYSIS

BRAIDWOOD, ROBERT J. *The Near East and the Foundations for Civilization* (Oregon State System of Higher Education, 1952). A brilliant study which combines careful archaeological and ecological analysis. Tries to appraise the general evidence in favor of the appearance of food production in the Near East and the sequence of civilizations in Mesopotamia or Iraq.

BRAIDWOOD, ROBERT J. *Prehistoric Men*, 3d ed. (Chicago Natural History Museum Popular Series, 1957). Written in a clear, simple style, this book will introduce the student to the type of social analysis utilized by the "new" archaeology in the realm of prehistoric man.

CHILDE, V. GORDON. *What Is History?* (Abelard-Schuman, 1953). Discusses different approaches to history and claims that the social analysis of material factors is basic to an understanding of history.

CHILDE, V. GORDON. *Social Evolution* (World, 1963). Another attempt by the famous archaeologist to argue his thesis regarding the preponderance of material forces in history. Though overstated, Childe's views have had an important influence on exponents of the ecological school of archaeology, especially on Braidwood.

COCHRAN, THOMAS. *Inner Revolution: Essays on the Social Sciences in History* (Harper & Row, 1964). An important endeavor to demonstrate the effectiveness of applying social scientific analysis to historical problems.

History of Mankind, Cultural and Scientific Development, Volume I, Part 1; *Prehistory by* JACQUETTA HAWKES (Mentor, 1965).

History of Mankind, Cultural and Scientific Development, Volume I, Part 2: *The Beginnings of Civilization* by SIR LEONARD WOOLLEY (Mentor, 1965). An important recent attempt by Woolley, to apply modern techniques of social analysis to the problem of the rise of civilizations. See, for example, his chapters on the "Urbanization of Society" and "The Social Structure," as well as the chapter on the "Economic Structure."

KROEBER, ALFRED. *An Anthropologist Looks at History: Selected Essays* (University of California, 1963). For many years Kroeber, a leading cultural anthropologist, tried to show that anthropology can throw light on the problems of the genesis, structure, style, and configuration of civilizations.

These essays illustrate his approach to historical problems.

REDFIELD, ROBERT. *The Primitive World and Its Transformations* (Cornell, 1957). A study by a leading cultural anthropologist of the condition of man before and after the "urban revolution." It deals with the emergence of new social and moral orders in early civilizations. Robert J. Braidwood has openly acknowledged his indebtedness to Redfield's work in formulating the principles of "new archaeology."

WEBER, MAX. *The City* (Collier, 1962). A classic example of social analysis applied to a particular problem—the city in history, types, structures, and patterns—by a leading historical sociologist of the twentieth century.

FACTORS IN THE RISE OF PRIMARY ARCHAIC CIVILIZATIONS IN MESOPOTAMIA AND EGYPT

Prior to the "archaeological revolution" the understanding of ancient Mesopotamia and Egypt was, at best, scanty and biased. New techniques of analysis of archaeological materials, new understandings of social processes, and new insights into the literature of myth have given to modern scholars a better understanding of the earliest civilizations, but many new problems have been raised by this new, sympathetic approach. The fact that the ancient cultures were not historically oriented and did not, therefore, preserve records as we do, has resulted in great gaps in the kinds of materials that we should like to have available. For example, did "higher" civilization emerge first in Mesopotamia, or in Egypt, in China or in India? What were the relations between the various archaic cultures? Who borrowed from whom? And if culture borrowing took place, how so? How were the different cultural traditions transmitted, and how were they received by the borrowers?

Again, what were the factors that promoted cultural growth in the Mesopotamian and Nile valleys? Were the higher civilizations products of the work of a single hero, of an elite, or were they the result of complex forces that were impersonal and/or natural? Did the geographical and climatic environment determine the basic forms of the Mesopotamian and Egyptian civilizations? Did the availability of materials determine the form of a culture in a specific place? For example, did the fact that the Mesopotamian built mainly in brick, while the Egyptian used stone, extensively determine the possible forms of cultural expression in the two areas?

Thirdly, what were the ratios of material to psychological or spiritual factors in the composition of the great primary archaic civilizations? To what extent did the Egyptian *conception of the world* depend upon the fact that the Egyptian lived in and enjoyed the benefits of a relatively stable and harmonious natural environment, while the Mesopotamian lived in and suffered a much more harsh, turbulent natural cycle of weather, water, and wind? To what extent were Egyptian and Mesopotamian religion, law, politics, and art a reflection of their respective environments? Is it possible to trace back specific cultural forms, such as kingship, religion, places of worship, creation myths, and the like, to an original experience of the natural world? Or do these cultural forms develop independently of the material conditions? None of these questions admits of easy answers, but they are all examined in the following works.

GENERAL SURVEYS

BAGBY, PHILIP. *Culture and History: Prologomena to the Comparative Study of Civilizations* (University of California, 1960). This attempt to understand the nature of civilizations and to provide a comparative methodology for studying them, contains interesting observations on Egyptian and Mesopotamian civilizations, as well as other leading civilizations.

CHILDE, V. GORDON. *What Happened in History?* (Penguin, 1960). Here Childe surveys the ancient world from the stone ages through the rise of metal age cultures and thence to the highest achievements of ancient civilizations. He concludes by presenting his own views regarding the decline and fall of ancient civilizations.

CHILDE, V. GORDON. *Man Makes Himself* (Mentor, 1951). An account that emphasizes the crucial transformations from the age of food gatherers to the Neolithic Revolution, which saw the rise of villages and the domestication of plants and animals, to the urban revolution and the rise of towns.

CHILDE, V. GORDON. *New Light on the Most Ancient East*, 4th ed. (Grove, 1957). Childe traces the rise of high civilization in the Nile, Tigris-Euphrates, and Indus river valleys. Urban life, government, writing, and the creative arts are also described.

COTRELL, LEONARD. *The Anvil of Civilization* (Mentor, 1957). Attempts through archaeology to supply a history of the ancient Egyptians, Sumerians, Babylonians, Assyrians, Hittites, Greeks, and Jews; and argues that these people provided the initial stimulus for the rise of civilization.

FRANKFORT, HENRI. *The Birth of Civilization in the Near East* (Anchor, 1956). Surveys and analyzes the problem of the rise of civilization in Egypt and Mesopotamia. Frankfort reaches negative conclusions regarding the possibility of solving the problem.

HUNTINGTON, ELLSWORTH. *Mainsprings of Civilization* (Mentor, 1959). An important attempt to show the importance of geographic factors in the rise and development of civilizations.

TOYNBEE, ARNOLD. *A Study of History*, Volumes 1–10, and 12 (Galaxy, 1962–1964); abridged edition, 2 vols. (Dell, 1965). Toynbee's monumental attempt at a universal history of the rise, maturing, and decline of civilizations is now available in paperback form, except for Volume 11, which is an historical atlas. The student will find many insights in this work, but the sections on ancient Near Eastern civilizations must be used with great caution.

PREHISTORY AND THE RIVER VALLEYS

BRAIDWOOD, ROBERT J. *The Near East and the Foundations for Civilization* (Oregon State System of Higher Education, 1952). Provides seven criteria for establishing the rise of civilization, such as fully efficient food production, urbanization, a formal political state, writing, etc. In this work Braidwood suggests that the occupation of southern Mesopotamia became possible through "elementary irrigation practices which must have characterized the Ubaid phase."

CLARK, GRAHAME. *World Prehistory: An Outline* (Cambridge, 1961). An outline of prehistory from the beginnings to the beginnings of writing, emphasizing biological, cultural, and social evolution.

CURIVEN, E. CECIL, and GUDMUND HATT. *Plough and Pasture: The Early History of Farming* (Collier, 1962). A good account of the impact of the domestimation of plants and animals and the rise of agriculture.

History of Mankind, Cultural and Scientific Development; Volume I, Part 1: *Prehistory by* JACQUETTA HAWKES (Mentor, 1965). A comprehensive recent account which deals not only with material artifacts but attempts to discuss the mind, society, art, and religion of prehistoric man; it ends with the New Stone Age.

LEAKEY, L. S. B. *Adam's Ancestors: The Evolution of Man and His Culture* (Harper & Row, 1960). This book, originally published in 1934 but revised in 1953, is a good example of how the archaeologist or anthropologist constantly revises his account on the basis of new evidence; it deals with Europe, Africa, and Asia.

GEOGRAPHICAL BACKGROUND

Atlas of Bible Lands (Hammond, 1956).

MAY, HERBERT (ed.). *Oxford Bible Atlas* (Oxford, 1962).

ROWLEY, H. H. *The Modern Reader's Bible Atlas* (Reflection Books, 1961).

All three of these Bible atlases provide the student with valuable maps of the lands of the ancient Near East as well as other pertinent geographic information. It is essential that the student use such materials for constant reference.

ARCHAIC MESOPOTAMIAN CIVILIZATION

It was once assumed that Egypt was the most ancient of all primary civilizations. Now, most experts regard Mesopotamian civilization as having a priority over Egyptian. Many questions arise concerning this civilization. Why was it a primary civilization? And why is it also an archaic civilization? What accounts for its immense duration and its basic unity? Why was the Sumerian contribution so enduring? What is the importance of writing in this civilization and how have we recovered ancient cuneiform texts? Was Mesopotamian civilization as "insecure" as we have stated in the text? What were the main Mesopotamian contributions to world civilization? What is the connection between Mesopotamian culture and the material conditions of the Tigris-Euphrates valley? How did Mesopotamian civilization unite sacred religious and secular technological factors? Considerations of these questions are found in the following:

CHIERA, EDWARD. *They Wrote on Clay* (Phoenix, 1955). A fascinating account of the recovery and decipherment of thousands of clay tablets with Mesopotamian cuneiform inscriptions. The author brings to life whole phases of this civilization by means of an examination of these tablets.

CLEATOR, P. E. *Lost Languages* (Mentor, 1962). Provides a vivid account of how Egyptian hieroglyphics and cuneiform were discovered, deciphered, and what they reveal about ancient peoples and civilizations; good illustrations showing different kinds of script illuminate the text.

DENTON, ROBERT C. (ed.). *The Idea of History in the Ancient Near East* (Yale, 1965). A symposium on the way the Egyptians, Mesopotamians, Persians, and other ancient Near Eastern peoples interpreted their past. The essay by Ephraim Speiser is very important in understanding Mesopotamian civilization and its basic cultural unity.

GORDON, CYRUS (ed.). *Hammurapi's Code: Quaint or Forward Looking* (Holt, Rinehart and Winston, 1957). A good collection of articles that attempts to evaluate the role played by the celebrated law code in Mesopotamian civilization. From this the student will appreciate how scholars differ on key issues.

Epic of Gilgamesh (Penguin, 1960). A prose translation by Nancy Sandars of the most famous epic of the Mesopotamians. It is concerned with a futile search on the part of the hero Gilgamesh to avoid death and to attain immortality.

HEIDEL, ALEXANDER. *Babylonian Genesis* (Phoenix, 1963). A

complete translation of all the published cuneiform tablets of the different Babylonian creation stories. It contains both Babylonian and Sumerian material and attempts in a final chapter to examine the relations between Babylonian creation accounts and Old Testament literature.

KRAMER, SAMUEL NOAH. *History Begins at Sumer* (Anchor, 1959). Kramer, one of the leading Sumerologists, attempts to show the decisive importance of the Sumerians in Mesopotamian civilization and the history of mankind. He shows their pioneering in a host of areas ranging from education to religion and law.

KRAMER, SAMUEL NOAH. *Sumerian Mythology* (Harper & Row, 1961). A study of the spiritual and literary achievement of the Sumerians in the third millennium B.C. Most of the book is devoted to myths of origins, such as the creation of the universe and the creation of man.

LLOYD, SETON. *Art of the Ancient Near East* (Praeger, 1961). Surveys the art of Egypt, Persia, Assyria, Sumer, and Anatolia. It has good black-and-white and color illustrations. It also correlates artistic developments with other features of the civilizations—for example, Egyptian art with Egyptian religion.

LLOYD, SETON. *Foundations in the Dust* (Penguin, 1955). Includes a consideration of the history of the most important Mesopotamian excavations, and of the lives and work of such pioneer Assyriologists as Layard and Botta; a vivid account of the growth of Mesopotamian archaeology.

MENDELSOHN, ISAAC. *Religions of the Ancient Near East* (Liberal Arts Press, 1955). An excellent collection of translations from Sumerian and Akkadian religious texts, including the creation epic and the Epic of Gilgamesh. The translations are taken mainly from Pritchard's *The Ancient Near East* but are prefaced by valuable additional comments.

NEUGEBAUER, OTTO. *The Exact Sciences in Antiquity* (Harper & Row, 1962). By the world's leading authority. It is excellent on Mesopotamian and Egyptian achievements in science and mathematics, and shows conclusively the high attainments of the Mesopotamians in mathematics.

PRITCHARD JAMES B. *The Ancient Near East: An Anthology*

of Texts and Pictures (Princeton, 1965). An abridgment of the hard-cover edition, this is the best available paperback anthology of texts and pictures on the whole ancient Near East. The section on Mesopotamia is excellent and introduces the student to a variety of important sources of Mesopotamian civilization.

THOMAS, D. WINTON (ed.). *Documents from Old Testament Times* (Harper & Row, 1961). Contains translated texts from cuneiform, Egyptian, Ugaritic, Hebrew, Moabite, and Aramaic, together with sixteen full-page illustrations; a good collection of translations.

WOOLLEY, SIR LEONARD. *Ur of the Chaldees* (Penguin, 1950). A classic account of the excavation of a single Mesopotamian site, ancient Ur, by the world-famous archaeologist who conducted the various excavations.

WOOLLEY, SIR LEONARD. *The Sumerians* (Norton, 1965). A paperback reissue of a 1929 work which, while somewhat outdated, is still of value.

ARCHAIC EGYPTIAN CIVILIZATION

Many of the questions asked with respect to Mesopotamian civilization can also be raised with respect to ancient Egypt. Egypt has always exercised a strange fascination for outsiders as a land of magic and mystery. From the times of the Greek writers Herodotus and Plutarch, Egypt has attracted interest as a land of great antiquity and esoteric wisdom. Has the modern scholar been influenced by a host of preconceptions inherited from the ancients about Egyptian culture? To what extent was Egypt, like Mesopotamia, a primary and archaic civilization? Why were the ancient Egyptians so conservative and resistant to basic change? Why did kingship play such a central role in Egyptian civilization? Why did the Egyptians have a greater sense of confidence and security than the Mesopotamians? Why is the afterlife all important in Egyptian civilization? Did the Egyptians borrow at all or extensively from the Mesopotamians? What do the pyramids signify? What were the forces making for unity in ancient Egypt and those contributing to change? Has our picture of ancient Egypt been seriously distorted by the loss of many ancient records in the form of papyri? Contributions to the solution of these and a host of other questions can be found in the following works:

ALDRED, CYRIL. *The Egyptians* (Praeger, 1961). A brief but up-to-date account of the ancient Egyptians; arranged by topics and covering not only history but many other phases of this civilization.

BREASTED, JAMES H. *The Development of Religion and Thought in Ancient Egypt* (Harper & Row, 1959). A valuable older account of Egyptian religion by the celebrated American Egyptologist. Breasted overemphasized the ethical aspects of Egyptian religion and went overboard on the originality of Akhenaton. His work therefore needs to be supplemented by more recent interpretations.

BREASTED, JAMES H. *History of Egypt* (Bantam, 1964). This classic account of ancient Egyptian history stressing political developments is now partly out of date, but still valuable for its wealth of factual detail; it carries the story of Egypt from earliest times to the Persian conquest of Egypt.

DESROCHES-NOBLECOURT, CHRISTIANE. *Egyptian Wall Paintings from Tombs and Temples* (Mentor, 1962). A handsome volume of Egyptian wall paintings from tombs and temples, with many illustrations in color. In an informative introduction the author analyzes the archaic conventions that governed Egyptian art, interprets many of the themes of the wall paintings and shows their magical role, as well as their sense of technique, composition, and color.

EDWARDS, I. E. S. *The Pyramids of Egypt* (Penguin, 1961). By far the best account of the ancient Egyptian pyramids, it provides an analysis of the evolution of the pyramids from the early mastabas, through the step pyramids, to the true pyramids. There are interesting remarks on the construction and purpose of the pyramids.

EMERY, WALTER. *Archaic Egypt* (Penguin, 1961). A recent interpretation of the first two dynasties by a world authority; it advances a novel "racial" theory to explain the rise of "Pharaonic" civilization and is interesting and comprehensive.

ERMAN, ADOLF (ed.). *The Ancient Egyptians: A Sourcebook of the Writings* (Harper & Row, 1965). A good collection of sources which illuminate Egyptian history, life, and outlook. New material and an introduction have been added by William Kelly Simpson.

FAIRSERVIS, WALTER, JR. *Ancient Kingdoms of the Nile* (Mentor, 1962). A survey by an archaeologist and anthropologist of the political and cultural history of Egypt, Nubia, and the Sudan; it is good on the contacts between these areas and has useful illustrations.

FRANKFORT, HENRI. *Ancient Egyptian Religion: An Interpretation* (Harper & Row, 1961). A fine study of Egyptian religion by a profound scholar who knew how to combine scholarship with illuminating insights. Frankfort tries to show that Egyptian religion was not an incoherent jumble, but was rooted in the idea of a static universe and eternal recurrence.

GARDINER, ALAN. *Egypt of the Pharaohs* (Galaxy, 1964). A recent political history of ancient Egypt by a noted authority; now more authoritative than Breasted's *History of Egypt* not only in matters of chronology but on many other factual details as well.

MERTZ, BARBARA. *Temples, Tombs and Hieroglyphs* (Delta, 1965). An interesting and accurate account of the history of Egypt in terms of archaeological discoveries; good on hieroglyphics and on descriptions of individual pharaohs.

MURRAY MARGARET. *The Splendour that Was Egypt* (New English Library, 1962). An account of Egyptian history and culture arranged usefully by topics such as social conditions, religion, art, science, language, and literature. The book shows the impact of the eminent Egyptologist, Flinders Petrie, on the author's views.

NEUMAYER, HEINRICH. *Egyptian Painting* (Crown, 1963). A brief illustrated treatment of Egyptian painting.

PRITCHARD, JAMES B. (ed.). *The Ancient Near East: An Anthology of Texts and Pictures* (Princeton, 1965). Contains excellent pictures and translations of texts from ancient Egyptian civilization.

THOMAS, D. WINSTON (ed.). *Documents from Old Testament Times* (Harper & Row, 1961). Contains useful illustrations and texts.

WILSON, JOHN A. *The Culture of Ancient Egypt* (Phoenix,

1956). This is easily the best available synthesis of ancient Egyptian civilization. The author writes brilliantly and emphasizes both the unity and changes within Egyptian civilization. Political and cultural history are skillfully blended, and the 73 illustrations materially enhance the value of the work.

THE CHALLENGE OF INTERNATIONAL EMPIRES AND COSMOPOLITAN CIVILIZATION

In the period after 1500 B.C. the river valley civilizations of Egypt and Mesopotamia were challenged by the rise of new centers of political power, movements of peoples, and much closer contacts between peoples. This new situation resulted in the formation of a series of international empires and the beginning of a cosmopolitan civilization. In considering this development the student should ponder the following questions: What was the role of the Indo-European invasions? What part did such highland peoples as the Hurrians and Kassites play? What were the cultural contributions of Semitic peoples such as the Phoenicians and Arameans to the new cosmopolitanism? What new techniques promoted the rise of such empires as the Egyptian, Assyrian, Chaldean, and Persian? And how was it that Egypt and Mesopotamia were able to maintain effective links with their archaic traditions? For suggestions on these difficult problems the following works can be read with profit:

EGYPTIAN EMPIRE

In addition to the works by Wilson and Gardiner, consult the following books:

COTTRELL, LEONARD. *Life Under the Pharaohs* (Grosset, 1964). A portrayal of Egyptian life in the imperial age showing the splendor and pomp of the pharaohs and the new cosmopolitan tendencies; it is certain to hold the student's interest.

DESROCHES-NOBLECOURT, CHRISTIANE. *Tutankhamen* (Doubleday, 1965). A description of the life and age of this pharaoh.

It is well illustrated, with a good account of religious practices.

PIANKOFF, ALEXANDER. *The Shrines of Tut-Ankh-Amon* (Harper
& Row, 1962). A translation of the hieroglyphic texts inscribed on the four gold-encrusted shrines that enclosed the
sarcophagus of Tut-Ankh-Amon, a pharaoh of Egypt in the
fourteenth century B.C. The text, extensive introduction, and
illustrations show the student the power of traditional
Egyptian religion in the period of the empire.

STEINDORFF, GEORGE and KEITH SEELE. *When Egypt Ruled the
East* (Phoenix, 1963). Originally written by Steindorff, this
work has been recently revised by the eminent Egyptologist
Keith Seele and provides an authoritative account of the
Egyptian Empire. Good sections on the conquests of
Thut-mose III and the age of the Ramessids, along with
numerous illustrations, splendidly convey the power of the
Egyptian Empire.

HITTITES

GURNEY, O. R. *The Hittites* (Penguin, 1961). A summary by a
world authority of the political, artistic, and social-legal
achievements of this important people of Asia Minor. There
are also good sections on Hittite religion and literature.

HURRIANS AND KASSITES

MOSCATI, SABATINO. *The Face of the Ancient Orient* (Anchor,
1962). A brief but suggestive account of the Hurrian problem is contained in this work.

PHOENICIANS

HARDEN, DONALD. *The Phoenicians* (Praeger, 1962). A good
account not only of the Phoenicians in their homeland, but
of Phoenician expansion overseas. Also covers their commerce, trade, explorations, industry, towns, and language and
shows the international role played by this remarkable people.

ARAMEANS

MOSCATI, SABATINO. *Ancient Semitic Civilizations* (Capricorn,
1960). Contains a brief but good section on the contribu-

tions of the Arameans and their role as international land traders.

ASSYRIANS AND CHALDEANS

MOSCATI, SABATINO. *The Face of the Ancient Orient* (Anchor, 1962). An analysis of the history, religious structure, literary genres, and artistic types of these peoples.

PERSIANS

DUCHESNE-GUILLEMIN, JACQUES. *Hymns of Zarathustra* (Beacon, 1963). A fine translation of Zoroaster's teachings in the form known as the Gathas, along with a valuable introduction on the nature of the religion and its impact. In addition each section of the Gathas is accompanied by a commentary that helps explain the meaning of the text.

GHIRSHMAN, IRAN R. (Penguin, 1962). An account of ancient Persia from its beginnings, through the Persian Empire. The author also deals with later Persian developments under the Parthians and Sassanians and ends with the transformation of Iranian civilization by the Moslem conquest in the seventh century A.D.

MASANI, RUSTOM. *Zoroastrianism: The Religion of the Good Life* (Collier, 1938). An interesting description of this religion by a present-day believer.

OLMSTEAD, ALBERT T. *History of the Persian Empire* (Phoenix, 1948). An excellent detailed account of every phase of the Persian Empire—political, administrative, and religious—by a noted authority. From it the student will derive a keen awareness of the international contacts and cultural influences that characterized the ancient Near East.

RINGGREN, HELMER. *The Faith of Qumran: Theology of the Dead Sea Scrolls* (Fortress Press, 1963). Contains a brief but judicious statement on the Iranian influence upon the Dead Sea Scrolls.

TARN, WILLIAM. *Hellenistic Civilisation* (World Publishing Co., 1961). Good on the Hellenistic legacy of the ancient Near East. By an outstanding expert, it shows how Hellenistic Civilization syncretized Greek and Oriental elements.

INDEX

Adams, Robert M., 10, 16
Afterlife, Egyptian belief in, 65, 78–80, 84, 97
  Mesopotamian concept of, 45–46
Agriculture, in early Egypt, 60
  in early Mesopotamia, 16, 25
Akhenaton, 95–97
Akkad, 23, 24
Albright, William, 33 n.
Alexander the Great, conquests of, 21, 47, 90, 108
Alphabet, invention of, 91
  spread of, 99
Amen, priests of, and power struggle with king, 93, 95–96
Amenhotep III, 56, 93, 96
Amenhotep IV, 93, 95
Amorites, 25
Arabia, influence of Persian culture on, 109
Arameans, 99–100, 125–126
Archaeology, and ancient Near East, 1, 2
  compared to psychoanalysis, 2
  cultural-ecological approach, 10–12
  as distinct discipline, 3–4
  "new" vs. "old," 10
  revolutionary advances, 2–5
  worldwide expeditions, 3
Archaic civilizations, differentiated from primary, 22 n., 23 n.
  function of myth in, 5–6
Art, Assyrian, 103–104
  Egyptian, 69–71
Ashur-bani-pal, 101, 102, 104
Ashur-nasir-pal II, 100

Assyrian Empire, 90, 91, 92, 97, 100–104, 126
  cultural continuity with Babylonians, 102
Assyrians, invasions of Mesopotamia by, 21
Astrological practices of Mesopotamians, 40, 44–45
Atonism, 95–97

Babylon, Persians' capture of, 20, 105
Babylonian Epic of Creation, 40, 45, 46
Babylonians, invasions of Mesopotamia by, 21, 25
Barter as basis of Egyptian economy, 60
Bedouin raids on Egypt, 81
Biblical narrative, and the archaeological revolution, 2–3
Bibliography, Arameans, 125–126
  archaeology, 111–112
  Assyrians, 126
  Chaldeans, 126
  Egyptian archaic civilization, 121–124
  Egyptian Empire, 124–125
  Hittites, 125
  Hurrians, 125
  international empires and cosmopolitan civilization, 124–126
  Kassites, 125
  Mesopotamian archaic civilization, 118–121
  myth, 112–113
  Persians, 126
  Phoenicians, 125

127